# *Socially* Smart & Savvy

**Top experts share their secrets for success**

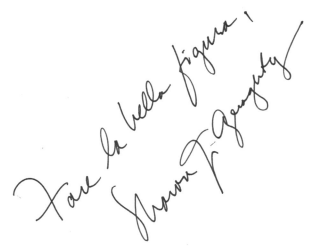

★
**THRIVE**
PUBLISHING™

**THRIVE Publishing™**
*A Division of PowerDynamics Publishing, Inc.*
San Francisco, California
**www.thrivebooks.com**

ISBN: 978-0-9850828-2-6

Library of Congress Control Number: 2012933684

Printed in the United States of America on acid-free paper.

URL Disclaimer
All Internet addresses provided in this book were valid at press time.
However, due to the dynamic nature of the Internet, some addresses
may have changed or sites may have changed or ceased to exist since
publication. While the co-authors and publisher regret any inconvenience
this may cause readers, no responsibility for any such changes can be
accepted by either the co-authors or the publisher.

# *Dedication*

We dedicate this book to you
the person who realizes the power of learning
what to do and how to do it in achieving your
goals and building a successful life and who
wants to make the right impression every time.
We salute you for embracing more knowledge
and we celebrate your commitment to being a
socially savvy individual.

**The Co-Authors of *Socially Smart and Savvy***

# *Table of Contents*

**Who Are You?**     1
*Personal Branding—Is What We See, What We Get?*
By Sharon J. Geraghty, AICI FLC

**Your Image Matters—How and Why**     13
By Toby Parsons

**Are You Ready for Your Close-up?**     25
*Best Style Practices for the Camera*
By Thea Wood, MBA, AICI FLC

**Savvy Interaction**     37
By Katrina Van Dopp, MAS, CHBC, AICI FLC

**Poised Under Pressure**     49
By Margaret E. Jackson, MA

**Business Smarts**     61
*The Essential Social Graces to Know in Business—and Beyond*
By Evelyn Lundström, AICI CIP

**Social Mixology 101**     73
*Meet, Mix and Make the Most of Your Connections*
By Rachel Estelle

**Styleguru Mantra for Solutions Inherent in You**     83
By Pankaj Sabharwal

**Influence—How To Get It, How to Keep It**          93
By Caterina Rando, MA, MCC

**The Language of Shopping**          103
By Shai Thompson

**Suits to Suit**          115
*How to make your suit work for you*
By Annalisa Armitage, AICI CIP

**Accessorize! Accessorize! Accessorize!**          125
Veronica T.H. Purvis, MS, AICI FLC

**Love the Space You're In!**          135
*Creating the Space that Reflects Who You Are*
By Linnore Gonzales, CID, Green AP

**Be Technologically Savvy**          145
By Karen Kennedy

**The Etiquette of Dining**          153
By Anita Shower

**Entertaining and Being the Gracious Host**          163
*Life is a Celebration!*
By Sharon Ringiér, PWC

**Wine Savvy**          173
*Business and Social Wine Smarts*
By Jennifer L. Chou

**Self-Change through Self-Love**          183
*Manifest the Body and Life of Your Dreams*
By Kat Kim, CPC, ACE

**More Socially Smart and Savvy**          197

**About THRIVE Publishing™**          201

# *Acknowledgements*

Expressing appreciation is a key part of being socially savvy. Before we share our wisdom and experience with you, we have a few people to thank for turning our vision for this book into a reality.

This book is the brilliant concept of Caterina Rando, the founder of THRIVE Publishing™ and a respected business strategist and coach, with whom many of us have worked to grow our businesses. Working closely with many coaches, consultants and other professionals, she realized how valuable the knowledge they possessed would be to those people wanting to be more socially savvy. The result was putting our ideas into this comprehensive book.

Without Caterina's "take action" spirit, her positive attitude and her commitment to excellence, you would not be reading this book of which we are all so proud. She was supported by a dedicated team who worked diligently to put together the best possible book for you. We are truly grateful for everyone's stellar contribution.

To Patricia Haddock, who served as the project manager and editor for this book, we appreciate your patient guidance, thoughtful advice and genuine enthusiasm for our work, and we are truly grateful.

To Tammy Tribble, Tricia Principe and Barbara McDonald, our designers extraordinaire, who brought their creative talents to the cover, photos, artwork and book layout, thank you for your enthusiasm, problem solving and attention to detail throughout this project.

To Tony Lloyd and Rua Necaise, who made sure we dotted all the i's and crossed all the t's, thank you for your support and contribution and for making us read so perfectly on paper.

**The Co-Authors of *Socially Smart and Savvy***

# *Introduction*

Congratulations! You have opened an incredible resource, packed with great ideas to make you socially savvy. Whether you are an experienced business professional, a new college graduate just starting out or an entrepreneur building your business, you are about to discover how to maximize your image and leverage your contacts to grow and prosper personally and professionally.

Being socially savvy is much more than handing out business cards or knowing which fork to use at a formal dinner. It is about creating a consistently recognizable brand, communicating effectively, building a network you can rely on and presenting the right image every time.

As top experts in each of our respective specialties, we have joined to give you proven, highly effective strategies for social success. It is all here—how-to's for social networking, creating influence, dressing for your true self and even how to host memorable events and choose the right wine!

The professionals you will meet in this book all want you to have quality tools and gain the confidence you need to enhance your social skills and master new ones. We have shared our best tips and provided proven guidelines that can make you become more Socially Smart and Savvy in every personal and professional situation.

To get the most out of this book, we recommend that you read through it once, cover to cover. Then go back and follow the ideas that apply to you, in the chapters most relevant to your current situation. Every improvement you make in your social skills will make a difference in your life and business.

If you take action and apply the strategies, tips and tactics we share in these pages, you will reap many rewards. We are confident that, like our thousands of satisfied clients, with our knowledge and your action you, too, will become more Socially Smart and Savvy.

To you and your continued success!

**The Co-Authors of *Socially Smart and Savvy***

# Who *Are* You?

## Personal Branding—Is What We See, What We Get?

### by Sharon J. Geraghty, AICI FLC

WE LIVE in a world of illusion, and we are judged each day based on other people's perceptions. This is both good news and bad news! You cannot control someone else's perception. You can, however, control the image you want them to receive by being aware of what you are projecting about yourself. The best way to accomplish this is by knowing who you are. When you know who you are, you become confident, and self-confidence is the key to your personal style. From an inside-out viewpoint, knowing who you are shapes your personal brand.

When you grasp who you are, you can translate this image outwardly. As characters in a play define their roles with costumes and a script, you, too, play a role in your daily life, complete with your own appropriate garments and personal script. Your grooming, clothing and accessories speak long before you do. Your choices for color, fit and appropriateness help others decide if you are someone with whom they want to establish a relationship. This means your visual presence:

• Can help you accomplish your goals and communicate your vision and purpose.

• Must reflect your values while projecting your passions.

• Needs to convey your commitment to communicate an authentic visual presence as accurately as your words and actions.

As simple as the question, "Who Are You?" is, the response will require you to think about and answer many questions about yourself.

## Personal Branding—What Do You Stand For?

Your *vision* is the way you would like to see the world according to your beliefs and expected outcomes. My vision is a world where everyone is able to project confidence based on self-awareness, creating happiness and fostering harmony.

What is your vision?

Your *purpose* is how you see yourself in a role that contributes to the outcome of your vision. For me, my purpose is to act as an agent for change resulting in challenging assumptions on personal and social levels.

What is your purpose?

Your *goals* are the action steps you will take to fulfill your purpose by focusing your time and energy. Here are some of my goals:

• Become a keynote speaker on the topic of translating inner qualities to outward appearance.

• Create five workshop modules that empower individuals to become self-aware and self-confident on three different levels.

• Work with clients that are motivated to reinvent themselves.

What are your goals?

By identifying your *values* and *passions,* you can make more meaningful life choices. Your *values* express those qualities that are important to you and guide you in finding organizations and people who support and share these and similar qualities. Your *passions* are those activities that energize you. They provide a clear way of measuring whether or not you are in the "right place" with the "right people." By "right," I mean you are stimulated by your choices, and the people around you either share or respect your passionate commitment.

- My values are compassion, connection, beauty, learning and teaching.
- My passions are designing/creating clothing and accessories, porcelain doll making and costuming, interior decorating, watercolor painting, and reading.

What are your values and passions?

What do you stand for? Companies spend quite a bit of money and time determining the qualities their products and services convey to consumers. Their *brand* is what they stand for. By purchasing and using their products and services, you are dedicating your time and money to that brand and supporting their effort in continuing to offer these products and services. Choosing how you spend your money and time is your power as a consumer.

Now, apply this same process to yourself. Concentrate on your strengths—your natural gifts and talents. When you maximize your strengths, you work effortlessly. Contrary to the perception that there is value in addressing weaknesses, I believe, along with a growing number of career specialists, that focusing on strengths results in stronger, beneficial outcomes.

My strengths are innovative problem solving, effective communicating, close attention to detail, good with color, have a "good eye," artistic.

According to William Arruda and Kirsten Dixson, authors of *Career Distinction,* John Wiley & Sons, Inc., 2007, your personal brand is your "unique promise of value." People will come to expect this from you, and you will become known for it.

Start by listing all the similarities you believe you have in common with your peers and competitors. Then, list all the ways in which you are different from them. This will reveal what makes you unique. *You will be able to use this information to make choices that translate your uniqueness into your appearance and behavior.* Revealing your values and passions will help you define your personal brand, which will in turn, allow you to express to others who you are and what they can expect from you.

**Brand Attributes.** Brand attributes are the adjectives used by you and others to describe you. Assessment tools for career and self-evaluation are helpful in determining whether others see you in the same way you see yourself. My top five brand attributes are:

| Self-Assessment | Others' Assessments |
| --- | --- |
| *Entrepreneurial* | *Creative* |
| Self-motivated | *Entrepreneurial* |
| *Passionate* | Intelligent |
| Visionary | Enterprising |
| *Creative* | *Passionate* |

Note the words in italics. Three of them appear in both columns. The way I see myself and the way others see me are in high correlation.

If you discover that the correlation is not high for you, consider how you will make changes, so others will begin to view you as you view yourself.

An excellent exercise you can do is writing an introduction for yourself as if you would be introduced to a group of people. Ask a colleague, friend or family member to do the same for you and compare them. You will understand how others perceive you, and you can make changes according to the image you intend to project.

**Personal Brand Statement.** Your brand statement will remind you of your purpose, serve as a guide for life decisions and provide criteria for setting priorities. You can use it to communicate to others who you are and what you stand for. Make it be consistent with your vision and purpose, ensure it reflects your values and passions and includes your unique brand attributes. Create one sentence that will describe the value you offer, whom it is intended for and what makes you different.

My Personal Brand Statement is "Using my enterprising spirit, creative visioning and compassion for people, I support entrepreneurs and professionals by raising their self-awareness, increasing their self-confidence and translating their appearance into a polished presence."

**Personal Brand Profile.** Expanding your personal brand statement into a personal brand profile gives you a resource with which to develop your resume, elevator pitch, bio and website content. You have already created your personal brand profile while moving through the process of discovering who you are. It includes your vision, purpose, goals, values, passions, attributes and strengths.

Here is my Personal Brand Profile:

Sharon uses an inside-out approach to image consulting that results in raising self-awareness in her clients. She believes that the alignment of inner qualities and outer appearance generates the emergence of self-confidence. Self-confidence, in turn, allows for the development of personal style and in the context of the whole person—a personal brand.

*"Know, first, who you are, and then adorn yourself accordingly."*
–Epictetus, Greek sage and Stoic philosopher

Using the information in this section, create your Personal Brand Profile.

## Communicating Your Brand

**Visual Presence.** Creating a "personal style statement" will motivate your choices in clothing, hairstyle and accessories. Creating this type of statement involves turning your attention outward. This is different from generating your personal brand statement, where you turned your focus inward. Choose public figures you admire and identify those qualities that best describe them. You have discerned these qualities from the outside in. From your list, choose two or three words that embody the image you wish to project. With dictionary in hand, analyze the significance of those qualities by discovering exactly what those words mean.

In order to differentiate yourself, ensure that the qualities you choose correlate with your appearance and image. There would be a different perception of a person whose personal style statement is, "I leave an impression of elegance and sophistication" and one whose is "I project a credible and confident image." While they may each be wearing suits, the former would be in a lighter color or black and would be cut more fashionably than the later.

**Verbal Presence.** Learning to state what you want, rather than what you do not want, sends a positive message. Change "I don't like the way you are answering the phone" to "In the future, I would like you to answer the phone by saying, 'Thank you for calling La Bella Figura. How may I help you?'"

Imagine how you might transform your everyday conversations into powerful declarations. Whenever you find yourself using the word "should," try substituting "would" or "might." For example, say, "I would be grateful if . . ." or "You might try . . ." or "I am hoping that . . ." These phrases state your intention or expectation in a positive way.

In establishing your personal brand of communication, carefully evaluate what you say and how you say it. Your words will define you. Let's see how this applies to making requests, which is one of the more important times you speak. Here is a simple method to get what you want when you want it.

You, as the "speaker" make a request of another person, the "listener." There must be a shared understanding of the key elements of the request and criteria with which the speaker will be satisfied and by when. Be certain the shared understandings are identified and defined.

Father to his son: "Nick, please stop by the pet store and buy dog food on your way home from work today."

### Elements of the Request
*Speaker:* Father
*Listener:* Nick
*Shared understanding(s):* Both understand which pet store. Both know what type of dog food their dog eats. Both know what time Nick usually leaves work.
*The speaker will be satisfied if:* Nick brings home the proper dog food.
*By when:* After work today.

Lack of clarity will cause a communication breakdown. Without the above-stated shared understanding(s), which pet store may need to be agreed upon, as well as the quantity, brand, type, style, and size of the dog food may need to be discussed. An alternate plan may need to be developed if Nick ends up working late and the store closes before he can get there. Many considerations must be accounted for. Missing elements in the request will cause confusion.

**Non-Verbal Presence.** In all cases, your body language will reveal how your words are aligned with your feelings and can highlight inconsistencies if you do not own the words you are speaking. Body language either reinforces or contradicts your words.

Your posture, gestures, facial expressions and eye movements are non-verbal ways in which your body may consciously or unconsciously agree or disagree with your words in subtle ways. When attempting to interpret body language, be aware that many movements can be misinterpreted based on cultural differences and environmental conditions. If your thoughts and words agree, your body movement will follow naturally, sending a complete message to your partner.

Personal space and the distance with which you allow others to enter that space signals the type of relationships you have or would like to have with them. There is an *intimate* zone reserved for family members, a *personal* zone used while having conversations with people you know, a *social* zone for new acquaintances or strangers and a *public* zone in place for speeches and lectures. When these zones are transgressed on any level, you may feel a need to protect yourself as you may feel threatened or dominated. Conversely, a person invading or retreating from your personal space may be signaling to you a request for a change in the relationship by moving closer or further away. Remember, culturally, personal space requirements will vary.

Several facial expressions have become universally identified and remain consistently recognized across all cultures. They are happiness, sadness, fear, disgust, surprise and anger along with smiling and frowning. Keep in mind, it may be inappropriate to show emotion facially in some situations.

Clusters of body language signals will always provide a more reliable source of interpretation than single signals. Arms folded across your upper body may signal defensiveness on its own. However, it may also be a result of the cold room temperature. Crossed arms and crossed legs may appear to convey a defensive message, or you may just be trying to keep your balance in an armless chair while protecting your personal space in a cold, crowded lecture room. As you can see, body language also depends on context as these signals could have an entirely different meaning in different situations. Eyes, eyebrows, mouth, head, hands, arms, legs and feet, along with proximity, all play a part in the not-so-exact science of reading body language.

**Online Presence.** Reaching a wider audience is literally at your fingertips by engaging with the Internet. Your personal or business website is best offered as an informational, inspirational and motivational representation of who you are. This is your first building block in the online foundation of your brand both personally and professionally. Be sure your graphic and virtual identities are consistent across all marketing tools, either in print or online.

Facebook®, LinkedIn® and Twitter® allow you to network with large audiences, increase your sphere of influence and reinforce your personal brand. You want to use these tools to build a larger word-of-mouth network. Choose the tools that best serve you and your brand.

• Facebook is a *personal* social tool allowing you to communicate with friends and family. A Facebook fan page is a *business* social tool with which you communicate your business or organization's brand to fans in an *informal* way. I prefer to keep my friends and family audience separate from my business audience.

- LinkedIn is a *business* social tool that allows you to present your personal and company brands in a *formal* way on a premier networking site. I use LinkedIn to make my profession known to others to generate business contacts and contracts.

- Twitter is a communication tool. In a business context, you can announce special events, press releases, discounts and free offers. I use Twitter to remind followers about events I am attending or sponsoring or new services and products I am offering.

Blogging is about revealing your passions. Determine whether your medium is writing or talking and then write or video blog accordingly about what excites you. Your personality and expertise will shine through, and people will learn more about you. You will expand your brand. Remember, link your blog to your website to expand your brand profile.

## Maintaining Your Brand

Observe whether you are "on brand" at all times. Being on brand will challenge you to clearly, consistently and constantly choose to purchase, use, and by influence, recommend products and services you find appealing. Your online presence and professional and personal affiliations also contribute to your brand. By keeping all of these components in alignment with the image you are projecting, you will present a sense of congruency and establish a brand trajectory consistent with your vision.

As your awareness of who you are becomes more apparent, your brand will require periodic reviews.

- Consider and implement changes to update and evolve your brand. As you gather new responsibilities or offer new products and services, your brand will need to reflect them. Add new information to your bio and update your online presence, logo, font or colors. Consider replacing clothing, accessories, office and technology tools and other objects that no longer suit you. Clothing and accessories may need to become more age appropriate or brought in line with a new position.

- Acquire feedback from people within your sphere of influence. Allow your image to project your growth and evolution. Now is the time to reassess yourself and have others reassess you. Allow at least six months to have passed for people you see daily and weekly. Allow twelve months for those you see monthly and quarterly. At these points, you will be able to assess whether your newly branded image is on target.

- Review your professional and personal affiliations with groups and organizations—your social capital. If you find that attending these meetings and events has become an obligation or that you are not attending regularly, investigate other associations that may be more stimulating to you.

- Analyze your daily activities across the broad spectrum of pursuing your goals, fulfilling your purpose and realizing your vision. Regularly make at least one effective decision or perform one important activity that moves you or your business forward on a variety of levels.

Are you are looking for your first job or returning to the workplace after raising children? Do you want to change careers or employers? Do you currently own a business or are you considering starting one? Is it simply time to reinvent yourself? Discovering your signature style and developing your personal brand will contribute invaluably to your success. Begin now and realize the benefits throughout your life.

**SHARON J. GERAGHTY,** AICI FLC
**La Bella Figura**

(847) 514-1524
sharon@labellafigura.com
www.labellafigura.com

*L*A BELLA FIGURA is an Italian expression that means *to present yourself in your best light, to leave a good impression.* Owner and founder of La Bella Figura and certified image consultant Sharon Geraghty offers a total package of services in appearance, behavior and communication. She supports entrepreneurs and professionals using an inside-out approach to help them develop a personal style in the context of the whole person—a personal brand. Sharon is particularly interested in helping individuals reinvent themselves.

An effective communicator and relationship builder, Sharon inspires and motivates with a positive attitude and perceptive insight. She successfully guides clients in innovative ways through transition stages of their lives, both professionally and personally. She offers individual consultations and group presentations on a variety of life transforming topics.

Married for 24 years to a successful business consultant, Sharon is the mother to two, talented, adult children. She has navigated through her life in a way that has brought her a breadth and depth of experience that she shares with her clients. She currently serves as a board member of the Chicago Midwest chapter of AICI.

# Your Image *Matters*— How and Why

## by Toby Parsons

*D*ID YOU KNOW that your image plays a large role in attaining your deepest desires? Image can lead to prosperity in business or your dream promotion. It can significantly prepare you to be hired for your perfect job. Image can improve your marriage, attract a special person or fulfill other personal and professional goals. Your image holds tremendous influence. *Your image matters.* Image has opened doors of opportunity to me beyond my wildest imagination. Had I not cared about my personal image and the messages it sends to others, I would not be on the path I am today in my personal and professional life.

We are all at various stages of image development. Recognizing the cause and effect of the image skill cycle will benefit you. (See the *Image Skill Foundation Cycle* diagram on page 14.) Every time you master even one image skill, you gain another level of confidence and respect. Your newly acquired confidence opens doors of opportunity that otherwise would never have existed for you. The resulting new opportunity provides greater confidence, inspiring you to learn even more skills, and the cycle continues to multiply effectiveness and success. Effectiveness, confidence and respect equal success. Image may very well be the link that propels you toward achieving your goals.

**effectiveness + confidence + respect = opportunities & success**

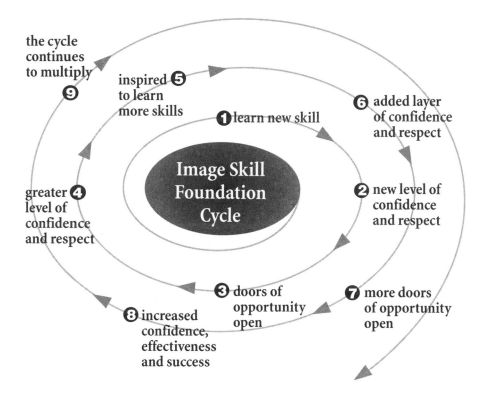

Consider the vast importance of first impressions. Your first meeting with others is not always in person. Often, it is by phone or in writing with an email. Based solely on what you see in person, hear over the telephone or read in email, you form your first impression within a matter of seconds. Note that you are forming impressions about each *Socially Smart and Savvy* co-author.

It is human nature to form opinions based on what we initially see, hear or read. Your image is speaking volumes about you, and it is impossible to turn it off or make it go away.

# Messages of Image

Your image has the power to move mountains in your life. You will never regret working to improve your wardrobe, etiquette, social skills or character. By picking up this book, you have demonstrated that you care about how you are reflecting yourself to the world.

- When you arrive at your destination, do you feel welcomed when your host and other guests stand up to greet and acknowledge you? When leaving, do you feel respected when your host thanks you for coming and tells you goodbye at the door? Yes.

- Do you think more highly of others when you observe good personal grooming? Yes.

- Do women with updated hair and makeup communicate a higher level of professionalism and typically earn a higher income? Yes.

- Can consistent application of design and fabric details help you to improve your marriage or attract a special man? Yes.

- Will others think more highly of you when they observe good posture and is proper posture beneficial to your health? Yes.

- Will wearing your correct colors make you appear healthier, more energetic and competent? Yes.

- Can clothing, accessories and overall appearance accurately represent and promote your business or increase your visibility as first choice for promotion? Yes.

The whole of your image is continually communicating many messages. Your appearance, etiquette, social and business skills are perpetual communicators. Your clothing tells others if you are conscientious, credible, trustworthy, approachable, authoritative, stable, confident, creative, sporty, elegant and the list goes on. As Deborah King, extraordinary friend, mentor and president of Final Touch Finishing

School, teaches, "Your image is either a bridge or a barrier to those you are meeting each day." You are forming a bridge if your appearance is seamless with your personality and lifestyle and if you are dressed appropriately for your daily activities, position or events.

Image is not merely the outward appearance. Character and values show up on the outside through your words, actions, grooming and clothing. As a wardrobe consultant, I must accurately capture my client's inner style. This is how I know what will and will not work for them on the outside. Once you express your true, inner self on the outside, you are free to feel fully comfortable. This communicates your intended messages and elevates your confidence. Image really is an inside-outside process.

While I have a strict client confidentiality policy, I can share some common threads. I will let you in on a few ways I have worked with clients and give you key results.

Women come to me for a variety of reasons. All want to improve their image. Some are struggling through life transitions. Several are over-whelmed by their sea of clothing. A few just need to be pointed in the right direction and want help in putting outfits together. Some wish to improve their chances for employment or job promotion. To suffice, they want me to make sense of everything for them.

After my initial assessment, I devise a strategic, yet flexible plan. I work hard to connect in a way that allows them to relax and see themselves, their image and clothes in a new way. Many client problems are solved through wardrobe edits and color analysis. I personally shop with my clients to fill wardrobe gaps, or until they are confident shopping solo and to purchase wardrobe updates or outfits for specific events. I sometimes simplify their life by buying entire wardrobes or specific garments/accessories for review and fitting in their home. My clients learn which styles best flatter their body type and enhance their unique features. I show them their best makeup and hairstyles. I teach them how to successfully represent their business or career. I give them tangible tools that help them on a daily basis.

My clients have acquired jobs, received promotions, their businesses have flourished, careers advanced, marital relationships improved and they have dramatically saved money. They have more time for their families, are able to get dressed with ease and can dress for all occasions from their existing wardrobe. All of my clients have increased in skill, confidence and polish.

A few tips:

- If your hips are larger than your shoulders, wear a lighter color on top or wear tops with upper details such as pleats, ruffles, pockets, shoulder pads, seams or prints to visually widen your shoulders. Use most of these same concepts on the bottom if your shoulders are wider than your hips.

- If your shoulders and hips are balanced, be careful not to throw the balance off. Use a mirror to determine what contrast of colors, fabric and garment details keep you in balance. Leaving a jacket buttoned or unbuttoned can make a difference.

- To visually lose ten pounds, go for a professional bra fitting. To visually lose another ten pounds, practice good posture.

- Benefit from smart wardrobe planning. Choose two neutral colors and three accents that are interchangeable to build your wardrobe. Begin with two bottoms, five tops, one sweater or cardigan and three jackets. This combination will create many outfits! Every time you add even one more piece, your combinations will multiply.

- Invest here. Buy quality handbags, shoes and outerwear.

Building a wardrobe that flatters your body type and reflects your personality and lifestyle does not take excessive funding. It does take knowledge. Because dressing oneself is seemingly natural, some women do not consider it an area that requires education. Speaking comes naturally as well, but we did not stop at the basics. We learned our first words, were corrected by our parents and teachers and progressed in fluency. Like speech, dressing, the language of color, body language and etiquette are also forms of communication. Your image progresses from infancy to arrive at the person you are today and to the person you wish to become.

It is vital to understand your personality style, body type and what cut of clothing works best. Knowing your correct colors and understanding proper fit are key elements to effectively showcase your image. Building your social and business etiquette and protocol skill set is another piece of the image puzzle.

## Your Image Impacts the World

Never underestimate the tremendous influence and impact that your image has on the world. Have you noticed the rise in casual appearance and conduct? In the 1990s, traditional business wear gave way to casual wear with the inception of "Casual Friday." Casual Friday evolved into jeans on Friday, and, in many businesses and offices, this progressed into jeans all week.

When you look pulled-together and professional, you are more productive and feel better about yourself. Your appearance has the power to lift your heart and attitude. Even seemingly small improvements make a difference. A lovely woman I know in Tennessee committed to taking excellent care of her fingernails. This small but significant image improvement has resulted in increased confidence for her which she takes pride in.

Planning and dressing with intention for every occasion will increase your presence. When I was young, each week my dad and I went to town, ate lunch at our favorite restaurant and did the household grocery shopping. I knew the preparation routine well—wash my face and hands, comb my hair and change from my play clothes to a dress and nice shoes.

Fast-forwarding several years, there are two acquaintances that my teen daughter and I ran into at the grocery store on separate occasions. One is a senior citizen and the other, a 30-something mom. Both commented that my daughter and I looked so nice. They both wondered where we were going. We explained that we were simply doing our grocery shopping and errands, and both women told us that they were inspired to raise their standard of dress—even for the occasion of running errands!

When you package your outer appearance well, you may find yourself treated with greater respect and attention by others. Have you ever made a quick run to the store, dressed a little—or a lot—beneath your usual standard? Did you feel anxious? Did you hope you would not run into anyone you knew? If you did, did you just want to disappear?

Here is a quick image check:

- Look at your handbag accessories, such as your wallet, credit card wallet, coin purse, lipstick case, sunglasses, eyeglass case and cell phone cover.

- Every time you remove one of these items from your handbag, others notice. They, too, are speaking messages about you.

- What are they saying about you?

## Image Increases Reputation

Regardless of your age and socio-economic standing, how you dress combined with your overall appearance attract certain types of people to you. Dressing consciously to attract the people you would like to know is wise.

Growing up, two women greatly influenced my interest in the power of image. Myrtle was a friend of my parents. She dressed impeccably, was gracious, refined, intelligent and treated everyone with sincere kindness and respect. She was a gentle, powerful leader who made a huge impact in her community, and many admired her. The other woman was my mother.

During the 1920s and 1930s, my mother's family lived below poverty level as Canadian wheat farmers, hunters and trappers. She used the skills of her work ethic, perseverance, award-winning smile, hospitality, kindness, respect, posture and eye for fashion to advance in life and become a successful businesswoman. These women developed skills and polished their presence so they felt at ease in all situations. Image skills helped them improve their personal, social and professional lives.

## You Can Do It, Too!

The good news is that anyone can reinvent or polish his or her image. If you have the desire and commitment to grow, I have some suggested starting points for you to choose from.

- Determine what your dress, actions and words should communicate.

- Build a wardrobe and accessories that reflect your goals.

- De-clutter your closet of everything that is outdated, does not fit or is off-season. This will save you time and stress when getting dressed.

- Put together savvy outfits that flatter your body type, portray your personality and are in your best colors.

- Recognize proper fit and what can and cannot be altered. Take time to evaluate and inspect yourself in front of a full-length mirror.

- Update your hairstyle. Be sure it is appropriate for your face shape, hair texture, body proportions and lifestyle.

- Polish your telephone voice and speaking skills. Pay attention to volume, pitch, clarity and speed. Read books about voice and speaking, work with a voice instructor or join Toastmasters®.

- Practice acknowledgement and listening skills.

- Discover and develop your personal brand. See also "Who Are You?" by Sharon J. Geraghty on page 1.

- Note body language. Learn to properly respond to the body language cues of others.

- Cultivate your etiquette skills. Practice civility.

- Develop a realistic exercise routine and schedule it in so that you will stick with it at least three days a week. Walk, bike, rebound, swim, dance, use an exercise DVD, lift a few weights for strength, enroll at a gym and so on.

- Practice smiling and eye contact.

- Plan and realistically schedule your time. Arriving on time and following through with commitments are marks of civility and professionalism.

- Practice returning telephone calls and responding to emails in a timely manner.

- Build your writing or penmanship skills. Handwriting represents elegance and education.

- Learn dining skills and study proper seating arrangements and table settings for all occasions.

## For Women Only

**Foundations.** We build our homes on a strong foundation. Shapewear and undergarments are the foundation that support our bodies, help us to smooth our weak areas and highlight our strengths. Build a strong foundation wardrobe that meets your needs.

**Skin Care.** A quality skin care program is essential, both morning and night. Flattering makeup that holds up all day is important. Visit department store makeup counters or meet with your independent consultant to determine which products best suit your needs. Check for makeup updates every six months.

## Avoid These Pitfalls

Image can seriously block personal, social and professional progress. Here are some pitfalls to avoid:

- Provocative clothing is a distraction for others. The results are usually that you will not be taken seriously.

- Casual, worn or ill-fitted clothing decreases credibility and could instill a lack of patient, client, employee or colleague confidence.

- Dressing inappropriately for your position can damage the level of success and respect you desire.

## Start Now to Make Your Image Work for You

It is not selfish to take time for yourself. Before a plane taxis for takeoff, the flight attendant instructs you about flight and emergency procedures. One action is to place the oxygen mask over your own face before placing an air mask over your child's face. If you do not put your oxygen mask on first, you will not be able to help your family or others.

I encourage you to schedule time for yourself on a daily and weekly basis. Give thought and time to what you want your image to say. Create a realistic plan and never stop working to improve the various aspects of your image.

Invest in yourself. Read and study, continue your education, take a class, attend workshops and seminars with your local, national or international image professionals. For poise, polish and life changing results, I encourage you to seek out the services of an image professional. Image consulting services are for every man and woman, are the fastest route to image mastery and quickly pay for themselves. Remember, you are your greatest asset.

Image is an ongoing process for all of us. When we learned how to ride a bike, we first had to learn how to balance. With practice, the training wheels came off, and we rode without having to concentrate. That is called mastery. So it is with image skills.

What one skill will you begin to work on this week? I want you to be the very best that you were designed to be.

**TOBY PARSONS**
It's Your Image
Certified, Professional Wardrobe
Consultant for Women

*Life is beautiful, dress accordingly*

(360) 877-5970
toby@iyimage.com
www.iyimage.com

*T*OBY PARSONS pursued an education to become a fashion buyer, and then she re-prioritized and stayed home to raise her family. When her children reached adulthood, she founded *It's Your Image* and became an associate instructor for the highly-acclaimed Final Touch Finishing School. One of Toby's highest passions is to inspire and equip women and children, so they may grow to the next level.

An engaging speaker, Toby offers a variety of public and private workshops and speaking engagements. Business and professional women depend on her keen eye for detail and perceptive ability to create wardrobes that reflect their personal style and lifestyle. She equips them to shine at home and lead in the workplace. Her clients delight in her unsurpassed commitment to them, and she makes a profound difference in their personal and professional lives.

A member of the Association of Image Consultants International, Koinonia Business Women's Association, Lacey Chamber of Commerce and Toastmasters International®, Toby is a certified wardrobe consultant and is certified in fashion retail and marketing. She enjoys family and friends, gardening, community music performances, quilting and swing dancing.

# Are You Ready for *Your* Close-up?

## Best Style Practices for the Camera

by Thea Wood, MBA, AICI FLC

*S*EEING MYSELF in my first instructional style video was shocking enough to motivate me to learn and apply best style practices for the camera. In the mirror, my look was right on and very flattering—on camera, I looked dull and unremarkable.

In today's visual society, you will end up in front of the lens sometime, whether for corporate presentations, weddings, charity galas, YouTube®, video conferences, speaker highlights, training programs or awards ceremonies. Mastering some guidelines will make you look effortlessly polished and confident. With practice, you will shine like a star and always be ready for your close-up!

## The Camera's Eye Versus the Human Eye

When working on a feature film, directors of photography spend a lot of time working with lighting techs, costume designers and production designers. That's because the camera's eye sees things differently than the human eye.

Briefly, the human eye's advantage is its partner—the brain. When lighting changes a scene, the brain instantly adjusts the color balance, so we always see green as green, blue as blue and so on. What the eye does automatically, the camera needs manual adjustments to accomplish. The camera's "eye" is absolute needing manual manipulation.

This means you can look better on film or video by considering the limitations of the camera's "eye" when making decisions. This chapter focuses on video, and most of the information applies to still photography as well.

## Choosing the Right Colors for a Healthy Glow

You have a unique "color impression"—a mix of hues based on your natural hair, eyes and skin tones. Choosing colors that complement—rather than conflict with—your natural color scheme will produce the best results on camera. It is a great idea to get a professional, custom color analysis, so you can remove the guesswork.

In my before-mentioned video experience, I dressed my guest in a blushing-apricot sweater that made her eyes, face and hair pop. For myself, I chose a brown and navy jacket and skirt that looked polished and sophisticated in person. However, it was so drab on film, I looked old and boring. Not a good look!

Here are color suggestions for clothes and makeup that will make your features glow.

**Avoid black and white.** Pure white is highly reflective and is typically too bright compared to your natural features and the rest of the scene. It can wash you out. For example, Hollywood costume designer Amy Manor uses the proven trick of staining an actor's white clothes with tea before shoots since the camera shows the clothing as white on film. Black does the opposite and absorbs too much light, which makes you appear dull. Portrait photography is more forgiving, but true black and true white are typically not a person's best neutrals. However, if you have naturally black hair, you have some leeway. The safest route is to find a neutral like brown, khaki, cream or gray, which are less severe and will complement your natural colors.

**Choose reds carefully.** High intensity colors may "glow" (appear reflective) or bleed into other colors on film. Red and orange are naturally very intense colors, so a tinted (whitened) or "toasted" (browned) red is your best bet, especially for lipstick. *Warning:* Wearing a red dress on a red carpet can turn you into a floating "head" on air as will any outfit that blends in with a scene's background. If you want to play it safe, leave the reds at home and show off your greens or blues.

**Gravitate toward neutrals and low-intensity colors.** Choose moss, plum, teal, peach and so on—whatever neutral hue loves you, wear it with confidence. Use the same colors and highlights in your hair and eyes and make sure the intensity matches them, so the camera can focus on your face rather than your clothes. For example, if you have sandy hair and sea green eyes, which are considered low-intensity or subtle colors, a neon green jacket would be overwhelming. The camera would adjust for the neon green, not for your features.

**Dress monochromatically to create length.** Wear a pantsuit, floor-length gown, top and slacks that are the same hue, and you will see the lengthening effect. While dark colors are known for slimming, dressing monochromatically is a way to wear light colors and still look long and lean. The lengthening benefits of wearing high heels is a given.

One last thought—a healthy diet, adequate hydration and plenty of sleep will enhance and brighten your skin, eyes and hair. Try upping your game in those three areas within 48 hours of your on-air face time for maximum results. Avoid skin treatments that may cause breakouts or redness within a week of scheduled camera time.

## Choosing Texture, Prints and Focal Points

This is a tough one because prints and textures look so different from person to person depending on facial features, hair texture, skin texture and body proportions. I did not understand how the camera interprets these nuances in that first video and wore a boucle fabric with a metallic thread woven into the pattern. Not the best decision—you will see why later. Again, you can learn from my past mistakes.

**Leave shiny things at home.** Sparkly jewelry and fabrics with a high sheen, such as satin, silk and charmeuse, are elegant. However, they reflect light and are not camera-friendly. Shiny materials also make a surface look wider, which is not what most of us are interested in achieving. For example, if you wear a sequined gown, the sequins will attract attention to areas covered by the fabric. This is desirable if you want to highlight your bosom, but counter-productive if you want to minimize a large tummy or bottom. Silks can be more subtle and drape nicely. Lipsticks and eye shadows also look better when matted or with a very slight shine. If you wear glasses, you may minimize glare by tilting them downward.

**Avoid tight, intricate patterns.** This category includes prints like herringbone or pinstripes and fabrics with ribs or complex textures, like boucle yarn. These patterns and fabrics cause a "moiré" effect, known as "strobing" in the high-tech realm. An unintended wavy movement in the fabric can deform your body shape. You may have seen silk dresses or pillows that have a watermark pattern to them. Those are intentional moiré fabric applications. The colors in these tight patterns can also blend, so the color you see on camera is not what you see in real life.

**Wear prints that mimic your facial features.** If you have a round face with predominantly soft, curved eyes, lips and nose, curved or circular patterns will work in harmony with those features. If you have a long or square face of mostly angles and straight lines, similar prints are best.

Some people have an even mixture of both. In that case, patterns that have both curved and angled lines are a good match.

These guidelines are useful when choosing and using clothes, scarves, ties, tops and jewelry.

**Iron your clothes.** The shadows created by wrinkles will show up loud and clear on camera. Take the time to iron or steam them out and stay away from starch, which makes clothing stiff, less comfortable and more prone to wrinkling.

**Keep the microphone in mind.** If you wear a lapel microphone, will the microphone clip scrunch up the fabric? Is there an actual lapel for it to easily grab? Beware of jewelry that makes noise if microphones are present.

**Choose a focal point.** Focal points are physical features or wardrobe pieces that stand out when looking at your entire appearance. When doing a close-up, it is important to choose one facial feature—usually your favorite—to accentuate. If you choose your eyes, try making them more dramatic by using eye shadow that matches your eye color or by pushing bangs aside. Wear a subtle lipstick shade and blush, so your lips and cheeks do not compete for attention.

**Use the same approach for your clothing and accessories choices.** Prints attract attention, so wearing only one at a time is recommended. Wear the print on or near the area of your body where you want people looking. For example, I am bottom heavy, so I wear prints on top to draw the eye upward and create balance. However, if I wore a leopard print blouse with a tiger-striped scarf, and my hair was streaked, my audience's eye would not know where to look first, creating an uncomfortable aesthetic.

Another focal point could be an accessory—statement jewelry is very popular. Again, anything highly reflective can become a distraction. Dark gem colors, semi-precious stones and antiqued metals are some recommended options. Shoes, bracelets and handbags allow you to bend the guidelines because they are farther away from your face. A rhinestone clutch or shiny satin shoes add pizzazz when you want it.

**Use a tailor.** Ill-fitting clothes distort body proportions and are uncomfortable. Find a tailor you trust and have them adjust any outfit you will be wearing on camera.

**Put your best foot forward.** Fix or replace shoes that cause pain.

**Use the proper foundation.** A professionally fitted bra and shapewear can transform a woman's outfit and her body.

**Not sure what to wear?** If it is a staged event, bring two or three options and talk with the event coordinator, director or camera crew. If not, ask an image consultant with camera-styling savvy to help you out.

## Highlight Your Most Valuable Accessories

Your face and hair are your most valuable accessories. Celebrities worship their makeup artists and hairstylists with good reason. Their $10,000-designer outfits would be dead in the water if the starlet's hair frizzed out, and her face shone like an oil slick.

Flowing, wavy hair will give you a natural, relaxed, casual look. Straight, sleek hair or slicked-back, tight buns are conservative, serious, hard-lined. If you are bald, ask for extra help with removing possible shine. Decide what mood you would like to create and style your hair and makeup accordingly.

Makeup artists and hair stylists will help you avoid all the risks. Let them know if you will be shot indoors or outdoors or both, and if you will be featured under spotlights or in a dimly lit room. Ask their advice about any professional or personal considerations that might affect your style. They will prepare you accordingly and give you the discreet tools for on-the-fly fixes when necessary. See also "Accessorize! Accessorize! Accessorize!" by Veronica T. H. Purvis on page 125.

**Tip:** Carry some rice paper to dab away oil in shiny areas and hairspray or a bit of hair wax for fly-aways.

## Strike a Pose

Again, understanding your body's assets is essential to a flattering pose. Here are a few thoughts for consideration.

- Few of us can pull off the super-model "hunch" successfully. The rest of us are better off using a straight and confident posture. First, it elongates your silhouette and neck. Second, it prevents the front of your top or jacket from creasing between your shoulder and chest. Third, it is healthier because it burns more calories and lowers long-term chiropractic and orthopedic injury. Excellent posture is also a natural sign of self-confidence.

- Stand straight and have a trusted friend snap photos of you from the front, back and side. See where you would like to make adjustments. As a general practice, pretend you are cracking a nut between your shoulder blades and imagine a string on the top of your head pulling your head up. At the same time, tighten your abs as if you are doing a sit-up—do not suck in—you will stop breathing and pass out!

- If you are standing and have a full-body camera shot, consider the position of your hands, hips and legs. Notice that celebs on the red carpet place one foot in front of the other with most of their weight on the back foot. This asymmetrical pose creates a slimming effect that appears graceful and feminine. If you want to appear strong, square your shoulders, directly face the camera and stand with your feet hip-width apart. Placing yourself slightly lower than the camera (photographers will place the camera at or above eye level) will hide double chins and bring emphasis to the face. Standing above the camera will exude strength and authority.

- Leaving your hands out of your pockets and relaxed at your sides is best.

- Many women are worried about their upper arms. Rather than putting your hands on your hips or holding the arm away from your side, wear sleeves that cover the area and forget about it.

- If you are sitting, mentally check your posture regularly. In a lifestyle centered on computer and television screens, we tend to hunch over. Shoulders may also rise as nerves kick in. A jacket's shoulders and neck similarly tend to ride up. Excellent posture minimizes this problem because your shoulders are down and back with your chin slightly forward.

- If you have great cleavage, and it is appropriate for the situation, lean forward slightly from the waist and do not "hunch." Again, asymmetry can work for you. Lean back on one thigh, which is easy if you pull one hip up and away from the chair.

- Etiquette books tell the women to keep their knees together, especially while wearing a dress. If you want to lengthen your legs, cross them at the ankle with greater than 90-degree bend at the knee and place the feet off-center.

- Rather than placing both hands on the chair arms, fold one softly across your mid-section and rest your hand on your other forearm. Another option is placing your left hand just above your knee and your right hand on top of it. There are many tips about how to pose your head and shoulders for portraits, but if you are on video, it is more important to move naturally, especially when speaking.

- Smile. This is the hardest thing to do if you are nervous or trying to drive home a serious point. A smile is perfect for most occasions and helps you relax. If you are self-conscious about your teeth, a trip to the dentist a week or so in advance can result in a whiter, brighter smile that turns heads.

## Practice Makes Perfect

Film and television stars train daily to understand their body shapes, movements, poses and quirks. The rest of us usually attend to other priorities. However, it is a good idea to spend some time in front of the home video or web cam and see for yourself how the lens is capturing your unique traits. If you do not have a video camera, practice in the mirror.

Try different camera angles, poses, hairstyles, makeup techniques, clothing ensembles and accessories. Throw on your favorite music, adjust the lighting and really get into the mood. It is like being ten years old again and playing dress-up.

Have as much fun with it as possible, so you become more and more comfortable. I am a big believer in signature styling, which is styling with your personality and a specific message in mind. See also "Tailoring to Suit Your Personality" by Annalisa Armitage, AICI CIP on page 115.

Stay true to your signature style while applying all these camera-friendly tips. This will have a very real, positive effect when it is time to make your entrance in front of public cameras and crowds.

## That's a Wrap

We have covered a lot of ground in this chapter that—hopefully—you will find useful. To make it easy, answer the following questions before airtime:

- Am I wearing neutrals and colors that work in harmony with my natural color impression and with the camera's limitations?

- Do I have a focal point in my outfit and makeup?

- Is there anything like a print or material that is too shiny or complicated for the camera to process properly? This includes my makeup.

- How are my posture and my positioning while standing or sitting?

- Am I comfortable? What do I need to address or change to be free of wardrobe distractions?

- Do I have my rice paper, powder and hairspray or hair wax?

- Am I drinking enough water and eating right? Am I getting enough sleep?

- Is my style appropriate for the environment, the situation and the message I want to send?

May these style tips help you feel like a star in front of the camera. Now, get ready for your close-up!

**THEA WOOD,** MBA, AICI FLC
**Austin's Signature Stylist**

(512) 217-9869
thea@theawood.com
www.theawood.com

*T*HEA WOOD experienced a major transition in mind, body and spirit with the birth of her son. She struggled to find a career and personal style that matched her new body, values and goals. Becoming an image consultant was the result of that process of self-discovery, which has led to a fulfilling career in helping others do the same.

Working with professionals from the entertainment and high-tech industries to stay-at-home moms, Thea helps clients create a "Signature Style," aligning their personalities and lifestyles with their physical attributes for a look that reflects who they are and where they are going. Her training in color analysis and theory led to a special interest in styling for the camera.

Thea is an active member of the Association of Image Consultants International® and is the association's international newsletter editor. She's "Style for Hire" trained with Stacy London and is a graduate of Stoltz Image™ Institute. She has a master's of business administration from George Mason University and a bachelor of arts degree from Ohio Wesleyan University, where she joined Kappa Alpha Theta. Thea also co-chairs the University of Texas Club Women's Organization and is a member of ReelWomen.Org®.

# *Savvy* Interaction

by Katrina Van Dopp, MAS, CHBC, AICI FLC

*E*VERYONE has heard the old saying *you have 30 seconds to make a good impression*–that applies to your physical image, what you are wearing, how your hair looks and, if female, how you are wearing your makeup.

What first impression does your verbal image make? How does your personality come out in your communications with others? In other words, who are you on the inside?

There are many books on how to increase your "savviness quotient" when it comes to your physical image. Why not explore the other portion of your image? Often, words can make or break a situation, compel people to pay attention or chase away potential business.

> *"Your words have incredible power. The words you say can change and save lives, but they can also destroy them."*
> –Kevin Baker, PhD, American pastor Oakdale Emory United Methodist Church

Have you ever thought, *Why can't everyone just be more like me and then it would be easy to function on a daily basis?* Yet, think how boring that would be!

The reason people act differently is that people have different personality styles. You can say the same thing to several people and each person will hear something different. Once you understand how to relate to others and speak their language, it will be easier to meet the needs of other people.

I first discovered the human behavioral model in this chapter in the 1990s at a conference I was attending. It was like being handed a universal translator! What I learned and have expanded on since has opened up an entirely new world to me. I began to understand who I was, why I acted the way I did, and why I related to my family, friends and colleagues in a certain way. I began to understand others, too. I became comfortable with myself, which has led me to be more successful interacting with and meeting the needs of others on a personal and a professional level and in a variety of settings. I have increased my verbal savviness quotient.

## My "Aha!" Moment

You must be clear about your own identity, your purpose and your passions to inspire others. Learning about your personality style will teach you how you communicate and why you relate, think and act the way you do. Knowing your unique personality style will also give you a strategy for how to address the needs of others based on how your personality interacts with theirs.

Betsy was a client in search of her identity. A physician assistant, she was not respected by her non-medical manager. After updating her wardrobe to a more current professional style, we talked about how to gain this respect. Betsy's personality was supportive or people oriented while her manager was domineering and questioning or task oriented. By recognizing these patterns and adapting a strategy tailored to specifics and bottom line results, Betsy began to gain her manager's respect because she was meeting his needs in his personality style.

One of the biggest benefits of learning this simple group of patterns is they boost your self-confidence in understanding yourself and others. A number of years ago, I was the wallflower at the party. I would hide in a corner until someone sought me out. I also was the country girl, educated in brain, but not in people. Four years at an exclusive woman's college had given me a great education and no social skills. Yet, to be socially savvy is crucial to daily life.

I had my "aha!" moment a few years ago when I suddenly realized upon discovering my personality style that there was a reason I reacted to others and spoke the way I did. This increased my self-esteem greatly. I did not have attention deficit disorder, nor was I unfocused. My personality made me jump from one project to another before it was finished. Now I have a relaxed relationship with time and get excited about new ideas. I was the inspiring, connecting and supporting one in my circle. Gaining self-confidence in who I am and who others are has made all the difference. *It became easier to work with other people.*

Had I known then what I know now it would have been a very different situation. Fast forward to the present—I recently attended the Bat Mitzvah of my daughter's friend. I knew the parents of the girl and one other couple there. Yet I conversed and intermingled with the other attendees quite comfortably. The wallflower was still around and now was controlled by my new skills. Suddenly, strangers were interested in talking to me and finding out what I did. I had become socially savvy.

First, let me give you a brief overview of DISC and how it is used in a wide range of situations from school bus drivers to senior attorneys. Then, I will give you examples of how you can use this information on a daily basis in your life.

> *"If I understand you, and you understand me, then doesn't it stand to reason that we will be in a position to have a better relationship?"*
> –Robert A. Rohm, Ph.D., American behavior specialist

# A Bit of History

About 2,400 years ago, scientists and philosophers, such as Hippocrates, began to recognize that behavior differences seemed to follow patterns. Many explored these patterns over the years. In the book, *The Emotions of Normal People,* published in 1928 by Harcourt, Brace and Company, author William Marston, PhD, theorized that people are motivated by four intrinsic drives that direct behavioral patterns. He used letters and characteristics to describe a person's tendencies. The DISC theory was born. His theory was focused on the positive, being objective and descriptive, rather than subjective and judgmental.

# Model of Human Behavior

Later refinements of this theory divided people into two groups. This model ascertains that everyone is either 1) outgoing or reserved and 2) task oriented or people oriented. The DISC model helps us start to understand others and ourselves. This is not to be used as a label or to highlight weaknesses but rather emphasizes strengths while addressing blind spots. Both are done in a positive fashion. Unlike other models used in the past, DISC allows you to understand yourself and to understand others in a brief amount of time. One is not better than the other is, just different.

- **D** stands for the Dominant style–outgoing and task oriented.

- **I** stands for the Inspiring style–outgoing and people-oriented.

- **S** stands for the Supportive style–reserved and people-oriented.

- **C** stands for the Cautious style–reserved and task oriented.

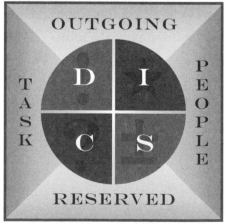

© 2005 Personality Insights Inc.

The "D" style is someone who tends to be described as dominant, doer, driven, decisive and so on. This person will focus on getting things done, accomplishing tasks, getting to the bottom as quickly as possible. Keywords when working with this individual are "respect" and "results."

The "I" style is someone who tends to be described as inspiring, influencing, interactive and so on. They love to interact, socialize and have fun. This person will focus on what others may think of him or her. Keywords when interacting with this personality are "admiration" and "recognition."

The "S" style is someone who tends to be described as supportive, stable, sweet, shy and so on. They will enjoy relationships, helping or supporting other people and working together as a team. Keywords when interacting with this personality are "friendliness" and "sincere appreciation."

The "C" style is often described as cautious, calculating, conscientious and competent. They will seek value, consistency and quality information. This person focuses on being correct and accurate. Keywords when working with this personality are "trust" and "integrity."

How do you see yourself based on the above information? Becoming a bit savvier about the inner you is only the first step. The second step is to understand others and how they communicate and interact with you.

## How Does This Information Apply?

You can learn to adapt your communication style to the people you are working with when you understand their tendencies under the DISC system. This information can be applied in a wide variety of situations from working with school bus drivers to attorneys. We are all human and no one is better than anyone else, just different. This is paramount in team building. Whether working with business clients or your family the tendencies hold true.

You may be wondering how this could apply to a group of school bus drivers. Their manager asked me to speak to them about how to use human behavior with the students because they wanted to relate to the diverse students on their buses every day. After I introduced them to the simple DISC model and showed them how to recognize style tendencies, they gained a means of understanding their students and could talk to them to achieve a degree of harmony while on the bus.

Recently, I spoke to the staff of a large church explaining the patterns and tendencies to them. A church staff is like any other business with a variety of team members. They do not always work and play well together. After teaching them the model, they understood why the pastor always had 100 ideas a day, went from project to project and could take charge, when necessary. I could hear the wheels turning on how to work better together.

## Family and Personal Relationships

You can also use the model in interactions with your family. Understanding their personalities better will make a huge positive difference. We all know that when we first meet our life mate, we are head over heels in love. Over time, what first attracted us to him or her sometimes begins to drive us crazy. There is a saying, "First you attract and then you attack!" Knowing the personality of the people you live with can help you handle the stress of everyday life. I am a blend of "I" and "S" with a "D" husband and daughter. I have had to learn to constantly adapt my style to maintain family harmony while teaching them to adapt theirs to mine.

# Business and Negotiations

John was an attorney who retained my services to update and enhance his image. He had just transitioned from working in a large, high-powered corporate firm to a college and contacted me to review his wardrobe and suggest changes. As I analyzed his wardrobe, I discussed his reasons for updating his wardrobe and what he hoped to accomplish. This new job was a complete change–from a structured business environment to a relaxed, laid-back college campus.

While working with him, I realized he had been using the model of human behavior to figure out his strategy in the courtroom without realizing it. What were his client's strengths and weaknesses, what were the jury's strengths and so on. As we worked together and I explained the four tendencies to him, he saw how he could use the information to help him work with his new staff and students to facilitate success. He had all the tools and skills to carry out the job, and he just needed to have a systematic approach for doing so. I followed up with him recently, and he has become more relaxed and relational, has lowered his guard and is successful in his new job.

Knowing another's strengths and weaknesses can assist you in every business. For many years, I conducted negotiations of federal contracts. Business is all about predicting what people will do, and contracts are the written tools to express what is expected of people and products with deadlines and expectations. Contracts are not the most stimulating topics. However, negotiations can be fun. This is where each party tries to convince the other that they know what they are talking about and can do the best job for the price proposed. During negotiations, I started looking at the traits of the people sitting around the table and realized that they represented the four styles. There was the one in charge, usually a "D," trying to convince me he was right. The numbers person was typically a "C," the business development was customarily an "I," and the program manager usually an "S."

## Marketing and Interviews

Think of the last commercial you saw. A good commercial will try to appeal to a wide range of people. A car commercial, for example, will often orient to more then one driver that the car is sporty and safe. While marketers may not put what they do in these exact terms, they are experts at using the model of human behavior to their advantage.

What about the most important form of personal marketing? Your resume has passed the screening test, and you have been called in for an interview. How best to approach it? You have learned your own style, so use that when speaking with the interview team.

For example, those in the human resource field are often people-oriented and can be outgoing or reserved. They are the gatekeepers whose job is keeping you away from the person who is the hiring authority. The more you focus on the following set of clues, the better you will understand what is important to him or her. Remember, you want to build trust with the gatekeeper. This will get you to the person you need to speak with.

Clues to watch for:

• Is the person friendly and talkative?

• Is he or she task oriented and interested in getting things done?

• Does the person ask a lot of questions?

• Is he or she quiet?

## Team Building

Developing an action plan to implement what you have learned about DISC into your business and personal life will benefit everyone. This is especially true at work.

The most important asset an organization has is its people. Yet, so often, they do not learn to work well together. Embrace the differences of your team—the outgoing tendencies and the reserved tendencies. Learning another person's perspective will go a long way toward reaching the goal of focusing on meeting his or her needs.

At one workplace where I consulted, the team leader was a dominant woman—a "D"—driven to get the task accomplished correctly. Her team disliked her and tried to work around her or ignored her direction. I explained to the staff how to approach her by giving her the details she preferred, showing her how the task is being accomplished, letting her be in charge while knowing you will accomplish your work your way and to her satisfaction. It worked. While it was never a truly cohesive team, staff turnover ceased and deadlines were met.

## One Last Word

Communication is a two way street and listening is just as important as speaking. One of our most powerful needs as human beings is to be understood. Learning to observe human behavior strengths will increase your listening and your verbal communications skills. Soon people you interact with will think you are the most brilliant communicator! They will want to be around you because they believe you understand them. Because you take the time to understand them, they believe you care. This is the first step in marketing—the client needs to know you care.

The personality style you project will leave a lasting impression greater than your physical image will. People will remember you as a good listener, a brilliant conversationalist and a person they want to know. It only takes three small steps:

**1.** Know yourself.

**2.** Know others.

**3.** Apply what you learn and focus on the other people's needs and what is important to them.

Start today to apply the three steps to ensure your success both personally and professionally!

**KATRINA VAN DOPP,** MAS, CHBC, AICI FLC
**Katrina Van Dopp Consulting**

(301) 570-5858
www.katrinavandopp.com
Katrina@katrinavandopp.com

KATRINA VAN DOPP, MAS, CHBC, AICI FLC, is a certified image consultant from Brookeville, Maryland. She is a graduate of the London Image Institute and has studied with Dr. Robert Rohm, one of the world's leading authorities on the model of human behavior. Since early 2000, she has been impacting people with her programs.

As a successful woman executive in a highly competitive environment, Katrina is committed to teaching others to be successful in their endeavors. Her unique expertise has led many of her clients to increase their success rate. She instills the philosophy that "What you think of yourself on the inside is directly reflected on the outside." She builds confidence and inspires forward thinking, so her clients can be successful and savvy.

Katrina has earned the credentials of AICI FLC from the Association of Image Consultants International® and certified human behavior consultant from Personality Insights®. She holds a master of administrative science from Johns Hopkins University, a bachelor of arts in history from Randolph-Macon Woman's College and a bachelor of science in biology from the University of Connecticut.

# *Poised* Under Pressure

### by Margaret E. Jackson, MA

*T*HERE ARE many aspects to being *Socially Smart and Savvy*. One of the most important aspects, and an aspect that will certainly get you noticed, is remaining *poised under pressure.*

Being poised under pressure was not a characteristic I was born with— but it was something that I began learning at a very early age. Some of this ability came along naturally with the progression of years. Some of this ability to be poised under pressure, however, was the result of often finding myself dining or mingling in formal, social or political settings. It was very clear to me at an early age that there was importance in maintaining composure, keeping it together and always acting like a lady.

"Acting like a lady" had nothing to do with the physical trimmings or traditional female behavioral traits. It did, however, have everything to do with thinking on your feet and handling yourself appropriately in all situations. Ladies were intelligent, helpful, quick-witted, gracious and positive. They were poised.

Once, after knocking over a pitcher of tea, I quickly learned that accidents, or issues resulting in pressure, could happen at any time. These pressure-filled moments can arise at a blink of an eye, and without notice. After spilling the tea, it went cascading over the table.

A woman grabbed her shawl and placed it on the table, surrounding and soaking up the tea. She then winked at me and quipped, "Thank goodness for this spill. I have been trying to get my husband to buy me a new shawl for years." Everyone laughed, quickly forgot about the tea accident and continued having a great time. This woman was most certainly poised in the face of a challenge (pressure). It was then that I realized that it is how we handle pressure-filled moments that makes all of the difference.

As I became older, I have learned that with a little practice, almost any situation can be handled in a calm, confident, poised manner. Remaining poised under pressure relieves tension and allows easier opportunities for success in whatever you are doing. Poise is important when sitting at a dinner reception, when overseeing projects or simply in day-to-day interactions. Being poised helps both us and the people around us feel more comfortable and at ease.

As the years progressed, I often found myself automatically chosen to handle the "stressful" situations at school, in my clubs and organizations and among my friends. For me, it was fun to see if and how I could deal with pressure-filled moments. After finishing college, I flowed naturally into managing programs and projects and dealing with issues and problems. My jobs required me to be cool and stay collected. I enjoyed this work, and it was the aspect of helping those within the projects that I enjoyed the most. While I continued to manage projects, I also began more and more to work with people in regards to handling and managing challenges. Out of this work, the Eight Steps to Being Poised Under Pressure were born.

These steps are a guide to be used and adjusted to fit your needs and personality. How they are used will vary from situation to situation. In some instances, they will work easily and flow well. In other instances, remaining poised under pressure may take a little extra effort. Finally, know that sometimes you will just have to vow to be poised under pressure—next time.

## What Are Poise and Pressure?

Being poised has nothing to do with and is very different from being perfect. I view perfection as an ideology that speaks to attaining *flawlessness*. For me, perfection is not something to appreciate or to which I have chosen to aspire. Flaws make you special. I like and appreciate my own flaws and the flaws of others. Flaws are a part of what make me, me, and you, you.

When I refer to being poised, I am referring to the ability to think quickly and be calm and collected, while acting and moving with purpose and direction. Someone who is poised gets the job done regardless of what may be happening around him or her. Earl Wilson, a columnist for the *New York Post,* once defined poise as "the ability to be ill at ease inconspicuously."

The official definition of poised, according to the online *Merriam-Webster Dictionary,* is "easy self-possessed assurance of manner: gracious tact in coping or handling." The definition of pressure is "the burden of physical or mental distress."

There are numerous types of pressures that show themselves in various manners. Pressures can be external, like bad weather or a traffic jam when you are trying to make it to an important appointment. These outside pressures may occur with or without warning and usually cannot be controlled by you. You can also experience internal pressures. Internal pressures might be the breaking heart of a person who has lost a loved one or a self-imposed pressure to accomplish or do well at a specific task, such as passing an exam. Pressure can come about because of various issues, problems or challenges.

Maintaining your poise as you deal with the pressures of your life is important, regardless of the source of the pressure. This is true whether you are a stay-at-home mom, a corporate CEO, an employee at a busy retail store or an entrepreneur trying to manage various deadlines. Everyone has to deal with life and its various pressures. Failing to deal with the pressures can affect health, work and relationships. A visual that we are all familiar with is a pot full of steam—pressure—that blows its top. Our desire is to handle pressures effectively and not cover them up, so we do not "blow our tops!"

Being poised allows you to handle pressures and use them to your advantage.

> *"Oaks grow strong in contrary winds and diamonds are made under pressure."*
> —Peter Marshall, American television actor and host

## The Eight Steps to Handling Pressure with Poise

**Step One. Be ready!** Pressure is everywhere. There is always pressure of some sort waiting around the next corner.

The number one way to deal with this fact is to be ready for it. You, however, do not know what pressures are coming. As a result, being ready is not so much a physical action, but more of a prepared mental state. Think and plan for the positive and be aware that, at any moment, you may have to adjust your positive thoughts and plans to deal with a challenge.

Pressures are an unavoidable part of your life, so do not be afraid of them. Think of them as surprises that keep you on your toes and test your abilities. They make you who you are.

*"Where there is no struggle, there is no strength."*
—Oprah Winfrey, African American businesswoman and actress

**Step Two. Make a choice about your attitude.** Choose how you will respond when faced with pressures. Your attitude is your choice. In some cases, you may first and without thought, react instinctively. There is nothing you can do about this. After that initial reaction, however, you have the ability to choose how you will allow the pressures to affect you. Ask yourself the following questions as you start to make your choice.

- Is this your issue to deal with? Is this issue or pressure your responsibility? Is it something that you need to address? Is it possible that someone else should be and/or is taking care of the situation?

- Is this an internal or external pressure? Is the pressure coming from an outside force, and is it something over which you have little or no control? Are there aspects of this pressure that you can maneuver? Is the pressure something that is internal and inside of you? Is it something over which you have dominion and can choose to handle in a particular way?

- Can this pressure or situation be turned into a positive? The immediate ramifications of the situation may seem to be entirely negative. Upon closer look, is there anything positive that can come from the situation? For example, are you hosting an event where the microphone system is terrible, requiring you to move everyone close together and create a more intimate and less formal event? Does everyone, including you, benefit more from the new setting?

- Is this really the end of the world? Will you live through this problem or issue? It may be difficult, challenging or embarrassing, and it is probably not the end of the world.

Think about your answers and then make a choice regarding your attitude. Making the choice to have a positive, "can-do" attitude will take you a long way in handling the situation and remaining poised.

**Step Three. Acknowledge the pressure you feel.** Once an issue or challenge presents itself, do not try to ignore it or pretend that it simply does not exist. We sometimes feel that if we do not acknowledge an issue or challenge, it will just go away. As a child, I remember covering my eyes and thinking that whatever was in front of me would disappear and when I removed my hands, it would be gone.

Your challenges usually do not just disappear (no matter how long you close or cover your eyes). You must face and deal with them. To deal with them, you must first acknowledge to yourself that they exist.

**Step Four. Acknowledge the pressure to others.** You may have a challenge that you think is apparent to all and extremely obvious. On the other hand, you may think that you are faced with a challenge of which no one is aware. In either situation, it is best to share your pressure even if you do not share all of the facts.

Acknowledging your challenge to the outside world puts everyone on notice to what is happening. One of the most difficult issues to deal with is one where everyone has his or her own version, thoughts or beliefs about what is occurring. If possible, always acknowledge the pressures being experienced to those that in some way may be affected.

Last year, I had to give a speech and moderate a program with more than 100 participants. This occurred less than two months after the death of a family member. The timing made this event one of the hardest things I ever had to do, and I was not sure how poised under the pressure I could be. I decided to take my own advice, so prior to starting the speech, I asked my audience to bear with me. I explained the situation, giving only the details necessary. I let it sink in. I knew there could possibly be times where I would falter, so I then smiled and mentioned that I did not want them to worry if I hesitated or took some time every now and then throughout our program. I told them that if I did so, it was only because I was listening for special instructions from my private angel. We laughed— and I began the program.

Had I not explained the situation and gone on to have moments where I paused and needed to pull myself together, the attendees may have thought that I did not know what was going on, did not know the subject matter, or had some other issue. Acknowledging the pressure puts us all on the same page.

**Step Five. Evaluate the situation.** When you are faced with a pressure-filled situation, it is important to evaluate and get a full picture of what is occurring.

- Who—Who does this issue affect?

- What—What steps need to be taken to address this issue?

- When—When does this have to be handled? Is it urgent or can it wait?

- Where—Where are the resources needed to handle this issue?

- Why—Why did this happen? This can be important during or after the moment or project.

In some instances, you may find that you have the luxury of time to review and analyze the situation. At other times, only a quick review and analysis is possible. Regardless, the situation must be evaluated. You cannot remain poised if you are not fully aware of the who, what, when, where and why. For example, if you are giving a seminar and the lights go out, you need to ask:

- Who is affected? Is it just the people in your room, the entire building or the whole street?

- What steps need to be taken? Do you need to check the circuits or contact the electric company?

- When do you need to handle this? Can you move the meeting to another room that has lighting and deal with the issue later, or do you need to address the light situation right away?

- Where are the resources? Do you know where the circuit box is or do you have the telephone number for the electric company? Where are flashlights or temporary lights?

- Why did this happen? Were too many things plugged in, causing a circuit to blow? Did the lighting go out on the entire street because this area has old wiring and power is often lost? Knowing the why is important for planning how things may be planned or organized next time.

**Step Six. Take control with a plan.** Once you have acknowledged and evaluated the situation, you are now able to take control. Whether you are taking control over yourself or the situation, it is important to have a plan. A plan is key to successfully remaining poised. It gives you and others involved direction. This plan directs your thoughts and moves and allows for control over the situation. Follow your plan and be purposeful with your actions and words. If you are confident, those around you will be as well. The fewer knee-jerk or automatic un-planned reactions you have, the better you are able to work at reducing and controlling the pressure.

**Step Seven. Relax.** Now it is time to slow down and relax.

If your heart is racing, your mouth is dry, and your head is pounding, there is no way that you can manage a pressure-filled situation. There is also no way someone will mistake you for being poised. After you have gotten ready, made appropriate choices, acknowledged the challenges, evaluated the situation and taken control, you must relax and take care of business.

To say you need to relax is one thing. Actually doing it is an entirely different matter. It is important to find a method that will quickly help you relax when you find yourself in pressure-filled situations. Choose something that is simple and can be done almost anywhere (if it can be done without people noticing, this is even better). Listed below are a few methods that may work for you and that you may consider trying.

- **Breathing.** Breathe in slow deep breaths through your mouth while expanding your stomach like a balloon. When you exhale, your stomach should flatten. Be careful not to hyperventilate, as this is a different way of breathing than many of us are used to doing. Do this a few times very slowly.

- **Visualizing.** Try to visualize something calming and peaceful that causes you to relax when it comes to mind. Linger over this picture until you feel yourself starting to relax. I personally enjoy visualizing water splashing up on the sand at the beach.

- **Muscle relaxing.** This technique requires that you tense up all of the muscles in your body as much as possible. Hold it for five seconds, and then release and let all of the tension dissolve. Try this three times. This technique has been determined to possibly affect individuals with high blood pressure. If you have high blood pressure or any other medical condition, please check with your doctor prior to trying this.

- **Counting.** Choose a number and then count up to and then down from that number. You may for example, choose to count to ten (1, 2, 3…9, 10 then 10, 9… 3, 2, 1). You should do this as slowly as you need to (taking into account your circumstances), to help you to relax.

One of these methods may work for you, or you may choose to adapt a version of these methods to meet your needs. If none of these work for you, do a little research and find a method of relaxation that you can use whenever needed. The most important thing is that you find something that works and helps you to be relaxed so that you can handle the pressures of the moment.

**Step Eight. Smile.** Last, certainly not least, smile. The easiest way to handle any situation is to maintain a smile. A smile changes your personal outlook and feelings, and it changes the outlook and feelings of others. This is the easiest of the steps. Try it.

These steps are the start to having poise in a pressure-filled situation. They are not designed to dilute, remove or cover up the pressures that may come your way. They are designed to help you have poise while you handle the pressures that will arise.

Sometimes, you will falter and fall off a poised pedestal, but that is okay. Remember: no one is perfect. Being poised is falling off the pedestal, getting up, brushing yourself off and smiling with the confidence that comes from knowing you are in control. You know what to do next. You are poised under pressure.

**MARGARET E. JACKSON,** MA
**Phenomenal Butterfly Coaching**

*Assisting women moving through life transformations*

(301) 686-8285
Jackson@phenomenalbutterfly.com
www.phenomenalbutterfly.com

MARGARET JACKSON works with women to create strategies for successful change and transformation. She works with her clients to focus on their experiences, values and desires. Her goal is to help them determine where they are, where they want to go, and the path needed to get there. She supports her clients in creating goals and strategies for living a life that is genuinely meaningful and purposeful.

Margaret has a bachelor's degree in sociology from Dartmouth College and a master's degree in education and counseling. Margaret credits her life experiences for giving her the knowledge and innate ability to work with women going through various transformational processes. She has experienced many intense challenges throughout her life, which have had a part in teaching her skills to navigate challenges and flourish with transformation.

In 2010, Margaret launched Phenomenal Butterfly Coaching and Consulting. The butterfly starts as a caterpillar and goes through intense struggles. These struggles, however, are a vital part of what helps this caterpillar to turn in to a beautiful butterfly. Margaret is recognized as a coach and speaker on life transformation strategies and overcoming obstacles.

# Business *Smarts*

## The Essential Social Graces to Know in Business—and Beyond

by Evelyn Lundström, AICI CIP

*B*EN, A FRESH-FACED banking hotshot, strode into the cafeteria, bursting through the swinging doors so fast they nearly bowled over his companion. He sat down eagerly and snapped his fingers to catch the server's attention.

"The usual!" he barked.

The server smiled tightly and took his order. Then, she waited patiently for Ben's now-embarrassed lunch companion to scan the menu and order too. Ben drummed his fingers on the tabletop wordlessly, scanning the room.

The meal soon arrived and Ben dug in, holding his fork like a shovel and not talking until he had finished and shoved his plate aside.

Ben was headed to the top of the finance world. He had learned the ropes fast and was likeable, well spoken and neatly dressed. However, he lacked social graces, and this was starting to be noticed by his clients, colleagues and manager. He charged into conference rooms or elevators ahead of others. He devoured his meals wordlessly, not looking up until he was finished. He faltered over personal introductions. His manager brought me in to "do something fast" about Ben's lack of etiquette.

That was how I found myself as Ben's companion in the above scenario, sitting opposite him and watching the top of his head as he ate.

## Manners and Etiquette—What's the Difference?

Etiquette is an oddly old-fashioned term, conjuring up visions of white gloves and "hoity-toity" talk. Today's powerbrokers—including Ben's employers in the banking world—know that etiquette is more than mere show.

Good manners speak of personal charm and treating others with courtesy and respect. Etiquette speaks of real social knowledge—an understanding of the tools needed to convey these good manners.

Think about some modern-day masters of etiquette—whether it's Michelle Obama, your company's CEO or a veteran Saks Fifth Avenue® saleswoman—and you'll also realize that those with outstanding etiquette also wield considerable social power.

Someone with good etiquette doesn't just open the door for their companion or know how to charm a host at a party. These people are fully-fledged social professionals—people who send timely RSVPs and thank-you notes, mingle artfully at functions, wield cultured knowledge at a fine dining occasion and present with warmth and authority.

The first step in learning about etiquette is to establish rapport with yourself, others and the setting. The next step is to learn some graces for life's key social occasions—including meeting new people, attending social events and following up with someone.

## The Three Rs of Rapport

Let's start with the basics of etiquette, which boil down to making others feel good. This, in turn, starts with establishing rapport with yourself, others and your surroundings. Here's how it works:

- **Rapport with yourself.** Think ahead to a social or business occasion and plan how you want to look, feel and present yourself. Be well rested, cool, comfortable, fed, watered, suitably attired and punctual on your arrival.

- **Rapport with others.** Understand what makes others feel good in a social situation. Whether at the workplace or beyond, learn to adjust to others' mannerisms or spoken tone by using similar nuances. Make sure to give a genuine handshake, introduce yourself with confidence and converse on comfortable topics. Give people courteous signals of what you are going to do. If you are running late, notify those who need to know.

- **Rapport with the setting.** Ensure the other person is comfortable with the surroundings. Offer refreshments, point out the facilities, clarify anything necessary about the schedule of events and establish some comfortable small talk before getting down to business.

Ben and I started with rapport building. It turned out that his lack of know-how was holding him back privately, too. He had been dating a special woman for three years and had approached her family twice with a marriage proposal. He had been rejected both times. Her family liked him, yet were worried their daughter would be subjected to a lifetime of social gaffes—such as Ben serving himself first at dinners, pouring cola into the champagne flutes, making abrupt departures or failing to introduce himself to new faces at family gatherings.

## Top Nine Tips for Working Social Events

Once Ben understood that social esteem begins with making others feel good, it took only a few days to put this knowledge to good use. He started by mastering the following nine rules for impressing at social events, both in the workplace and beyond. Note that we have created a separate section to discuss rules of conversation—a huge topic on its own.

**1. RSVPs.** Reply to an invitation promptly—ideally, within one week of receiving the invitation, whether or not you will attend. Honor your commitments. Don't cancel one invitation because another, more compelling one has come up. You risk hurting the feelings of the person who first invited you, and etiquette is about making others feel good.

**2. Setting a Compelling Outcome.** Get more out of a social or business event by setting an outcome for yourself before you go. This could be to meet three new people or reconnect with a former mentor or colleague. Setting an agenda will help you subconsciously seek out opportunities to fulfill it.

Relax if you fall short of your goal. Enjoying yourself is another prerequisite of attending a social event, so give yourself a tick if you have achieved that instead of collecting a tenth business card.

**3. Arriving.** Make sure you arrive on time or no more than fifteen minutes late for casual, social occasions. On arriving, greet the host if you know him or her and introduce yourself if you don't. If you have read the first rule of rapport, you will be neither parched nor famished and won't dive onto the food and drinks. Accept a drink and a snack and proceed to mingle.

On the host's side, note whether any new arrivals seem alone and introduce them to other guests with whom they may have something in common. Make sure your guests know where to find food, drinks and amenities.

**4. Quality Introductions and Handshakes.** Few impressions will stay with people as long as the first one, so make sure to get your introductions right. When meeting someone for the first time, introduce yourself in full, using your family name and company name—or your relationship to the host if it's a private function.

Introduce any companions in the same manner. Shake hands firmly, front-on, while making sure to stand up straight, smile and look the other person in the eye.

Make sure to address the most important person in the gathering first. For example, say to your employer, "Mrs. Jones, these are my friends John Smith and Jane Kwok" and then, "John and Jane, this is my boss, Mrs. Jones"—not the other way around. After introducing yourself and anyone with you, tell the person what you have been discussing and engage them in that discussion. Alternatively, ask them about themselves and what they do.

**5. Approaching Others.** Sometimes the person you want to speak with is with other people all night, and it's hard to get close. Try to join them when there's at least one other person in the group you know. Walk close to the group—someone will notice you. Make eye contact with the person and say something to acknowledge your intrusion, for example, "Hi. I'm Evelyn, and I haven't seen Bob for so long, I just wanted to catch up with him."

Sometimes, you may be lucky enough to find yourself momentarily alone with the person you've been seeking out—near the refreshments, for example, or moving between areas. Introduce yourself and strike up a conversation. If you're at a loss about what to say, ask them about themselves.

People at the top love talking about how they got there. Try saying something like, "I've been tracking your career—what would you recommend for someone in my position?" Make sure to follow up the conversation with an appropriate thank you (see below).

**6. Being *There*.** One of the most annoying guests at any social function is one who is there—and not present. You know this person—the one scanning the room while pretending to listen to a conversation or clearly bored with the proceedings.

Avoid becoming this person yourself by setting an outcome for the event. If you cannot find an outcome, don't go. Alternatively, embrace those moments where you find yourself alone. It is much better form to admire the art or the view alone for ten minutes than pretend to be interested in someone when it is obvious you are not.

**7. Handling Alcoholic Beverages.** If you drink at social functions, drink in moderation. If you cannot mingle without something in your hand, make sure you drink a glass of water after every glass of wine. Simply place a hand over your glass to decline a top-up.

At standing functions, keep your right hand free to shake hands by holding your glass, napkin and canapé in your left hand. You can do this by mastering the technique of threading a napkin between your middle finger and ring finger, so part of the napkin covers the palm of your left hand. Then clamp your wine glass between your forefinger and thumb and rest a canapé on your napkin-covered palm.

**8. Leaving.** Sometime after the end of the formalities, it is appropriate to leave. If you must be the first out the door, make sure to excuse yourself to your host appropriately. On the other hand, don't overstay your welcome and be the last out the door, either.

Once the evening starts to wear and the formalities are over, shake hands with those around you and say goodbye. Keep your goodbyes short and say you will be in touch if there is someone you still want to speak with. Seek out the hosts and thank them for the invitation, being sure to include a brief and sincere compliment on the occasion. Then leave. Don't get distracted by others as you leave and find yourself face-to-face with someone you said goodbye to an hour earlier, which will have them thinking you wanted to escape them.

**9. And Afterwards…** It sounds old-fashioned—a handwritten note or card is still the most gracious and elegant way to thank hosts for their efforts. Even if they spoke to you for barely five minutes during the occasion, they will appreciate and remember you clearly with this gesture. Email thank you notes are simply not the same.

# Top Three Tips for Office Etiquette

The basic rules for conduct at the office are not much different from those above, regarding conduct at a social occasion. However, for the record, here are some additional things to keep in mind.

**1. Quality Handshakes and Introductions.** As explained above, you should never underestimate the importance of introductions. Always introduce yourself and others in full and address the important people first. Pay attention to your handshake—it should be firm, friendly, last for two or three shakes and be accompanied with a smile and firm gaze. Get someone to review your handshake if you are not sure of the impression it is leaving, whether too weak or too strong.

**2. Conduct at Meetings.** The key to a successful meeting is to be prepared—just like for any social occasion. Before the meeting, read the agenda, do your research and give others enough time to prepare key materials. At the meeting, arrive on time, take notes and present the ideas you have prepared earlier. After the meeting, follow up by sending notes, web links or ideas to colleagues and acknowledge any contributions made.

**3. Mixing with Others.** The workplace is not just about boardrooms and workstations. You will cross colleagues and bosses in the kitchens, hallways, elevators and the taxi stand out front, so keep in mind the principles of making others feel good by letting people go first, respecting their personal space and keeping interactions professional and appropriate.

# The Smart Conversationalist

As with all etiquette, artful conversation boils down to making the other person feel good.

Stand at arm's length to respect the other person's personal space while still being able to hear and be heard. Match their tone of voice and seek out topics of mutual interest. If you notice someone trying to join your group at a function, introduce yourself and engage them in your discussion or simply ask about them and what they do.

Next, make sure the conversation keeps everyone feeling good by sticking with neutral topics like sports and the arts, current affairs, company policy, client needs, ideas supportive of the company or occasions and upcoming events. Avoid controversial areas such as religion, politics, your (or others') personal lives, gossip, management gripes and divisive issues.

Be aware of your style of conversation. Are you naturally chatty? Ask someone to tell you if you're so chatty that others don't get a word in. On the other hand, are you naturally reticent? If you are often stuck for words, try repeating the last point made by the person and then adding to it, rather than responding with mostly "ums" and "ahs."

Finally, learn to make the right closing when you feel it is time to move on. Instead of making a vague escape like "Anyway, I really need some food now," or "There's my friend Rob," acknowledge the conversation simply and without making excuses. For example, "Well, that's been really interesting, and I will certainly look up that website on marlin fishing. I hope we can catch up again." See also "Social Mixology 101" by Rachel Estelle on page 73.

## The Model Student

Mastering the basics of etiquette does not take long, as our determined young banker, Ben, discovered. Within a week of etiquette training, Ben was subjected to a critical test—taking his boss, Michael, out to dinner and dealing with a number of unscripted glitches.

For example, finding himself running five minutes late, Ben thought for a moment before calling the restaurant. He introduced himself and then said, "I'm taking my boss to dinner tonight, and he is about to arrive. Please seat him at the bar, take his drink order and put it on my account."

During the evening, Ben was a model of courtesy, inviting Michael to select the wines, serving himself last from the breadbasket, standing up when a female companion left the table and conversing with ease between unhurried mouthfuls.

At the evening's end, Michael signaled for the staff to bring the check.

"Thank you, sir, but your companion here has already organized it," came the server's smiling response.

Ben had discreetly paid for the whole dinner ten minutes earlier.

Ben not only got his promotion and the recognition that came with it, he also got the girl several months later. His change in behavior so impressed his future parents-in-law that they wholeheartedly endorsed his proposal of marriage to their daughter.

## What's Next?

Successful business people are a little like great athletes—the more varied their training, the better the results. Business professionals will project their success most effectively when they are cultured, well-spoken, stylish, fit, charming and etiquette savvy.

There are many steps—big and small—that you can take to improve your know-how of business etiquette, beginning with mastering the basics outlined here.

As with any kind of change, you will get the best results if you don't attempt to do it solo. Partner up with a learning buddy who wants to make the same changes, or get someone you trust to rank you from one to ten in the various areas described in this chapter. You will be surprised at how quickly a little etiquette training can boost your business and social skillsets.

**EVELYN LUNDSTRÖM,** AICI CIP
**First Impressions Image Training
and Consulting Pty Ltd**

+61 1300 889 180
evelyn@firstimpressions.com.au
www.firstimpressions.com.au

*E*VELYN LUNDSTRÖM is one of Australia's most experienced image and personal branding consultants with her company, First Impressions Image Training and Consulting. A certified image professional with the Association of Image Consultants Inter-national® and a master practitioner of NLP and timeline therapy, Evelyn develops and delivers training programs for industries as diverse as financial services, professional services, travel, hospitality and academia. She advises corporate groups and individuals on image management strategies for greater recognition and personal success.

A trusted advisor and coach, Evelyn delights in helping individuals improve their personal image, grooming and presentation style to achieve their highest goals.

Recognized as a preferred trainer of image professionals entering the industry, Evelyn has developed the *Definitive Colour Profiling System* for image and color professionals internationally. She is the co-author of *Executive Style* published by Prentice Hall in 1980 and is currently writing the definitive book on *How Not To Do Old.*

# *Social* Mixology 101

## Meet, Mix and Make the Most of Your Connections

by Rachel Estelle

*A*T ABOUT 8:30 p.m. on a Wednesday night, I walked into the hallway and locked myself out of my apartment. My cell phone, car keys and puppy were all inside. The third floor of a highly secured building is not easily re-entered.

The only way I could get back into my apartment was to use my socially smart and savvy skills. I went straight to Mark and Mike's apartment across the courtyard after seeing their lights on. I had made friends with them over the last four months. We exchanged opinions about clubs and restaurants in our neighborhood and then had quickly moved on to things we had in common. Before long, we were friends, inviting each other over for parties.

Mark was home and let me in to use his cell phone. After no response from the locksmith or the leasing office's "emergency line," I felt deflated. I left Mark's apartment and went to Lisa's, who lived down the hall from them. We had met one day in the elevator. I complimented her on her shoes and we began to make small talk for the next few months as we ran into each other. We had become friends after countless conversations about clothes and shoes. I rang Lisa's doorbell—no answer.

I now stood in the courtyard looking up at my apartment. All the lights were on and Bentley was in the window, paws pressed against the pane, licking it. I could tell his tail was wagging feverishly and he was barking for me to take him out. I felt helpless. The only way I would be able to get to my apartment was through the windows.

How was I going to get myself up to the third floor? I would need the biggest ladder in the world and who would have that? My mind was literally blank. Then, a wave of relief came over me when I realized exactly who would have it. I left the courtyard, walked down to the neighborhood Thai restaurant, and asked for Steven.

I had met Steven about a year ago while eating dinner at the bar. I began talking to the bartender about the Pad Thai I was eating and inquired about the ingredients. Steven happened to be behind the bar too, and we began to talk about food and whiskey. After months of eating at his restaurant on a regular basis, I made sure I said hello to him every time I saw him. We made small talk and became friends.

I explained my situation to Steven and he offered his 24-foot ladder, which I carried to the courtyard and planted underneath my bedroom window. After a frightening climb to the top, I was able to take the screen off my window and pull myself up to the opening. I was greeted by Bentley, licking my face, as I hoisted the rest of my body through the window and entered my apartment successfully.

## Importance of Being Social

The helplessness I felt when I could not think of a way to get back into my apartment left me feeling lonely and confused. I hate that feeling. The only thing that empowered me was my social ties in that apartment complex. Having several people to call on, borrow a cell phone from, exchange information with and borrow a ladder from, got me back into that apartment ten times faster than had I started randomly knocking on the doors of strangers and asking for help. Just knowing I had so many connections in the area around me made me feel better. In a complex of at least 200 apartments, I could immediately think of a dozen apartments where I had a friend or someone would recognize me from casual conversation.

Most of us have been locked out of our car, our work, our house, our apartment. Most of us, at one time or another, have needed the help of someone else.

What was the first thing you thought when you were stranded? "Who can I call to help me?" More importantly, "Whom do I know that can help me?"

We all need connections with people. It is critical for our survival—and for getting back into our apartments! We all need people. In this chapter, I am going to give you the tools you need to meet, mix and make the most of your connections.

> *"Just go up to somebody on the street and say,*
> *'You're it!' and then run away."*
> — Ellen DeGeneres, American talk show host and comedian

## Begin Meeting New People

How do you start these connections with people around you? Most people seem to be so busy and so caught up in their own lives, it may seem as if they do not want to meet you—or anyone!

How do you become friends with them? Keep in mind, none of the people in my story were intimate friends of mine. I had to run into them dozens of times over months and had merely exchanged greetings.

Then, I began to make small talk. After that, I had to make an effort to continue to say "hi" to them even if I had forgotten their name or what we talked about before. Sometimes, I ran into them when I wasn't looking or feeling my best, when I was carrying too many groceries, engaged in a phone conversation or even when they were doing all of these things, too.

The important thing is this: *They saw me, and I always made at least eye contact and smiled to make an impression.* Sometimes, they did not smile back or respond to me. It is okay. It does not mean there is something wrong. It just means they were not in the right mindset to meet and greet. The goal is not to change them. The goal is to find someone who wants to meet you, too.

When I take Bentley to the dog park, not every dog wants to play with him. This actually makes *me* feel bad, yet it seems to have no effect on Bentley. He still runs up to other dogs, wags his tail and barks to get their attention. He is telling them, "Hey, I'm here to play! I want to play with *you*." If he is turned down by one group, he just moves on to the next group and does the same. He does this until someone lets him in their pack. I have watched him do this repeatedly, and I admire his persistence. He has actually taught me a little about how to socialize. He does not take it personally, he just moves on with the same enthusiasm. If you do not have the luxury of going to a "fenced in, people park" to play with new people, or you do not live in a big apartment complex as I do, or let's be extreme and say you have no neighbors and live somewhere remote, *you can still meet people!*

> **"The road to success is always under construction."**
> — *Lily Tomlin, American actress and comedian*

Start with the people who are closest to you. I do not necessarily mean people who physically live the closest to you. I mean people who share the same hobbies, interests or pets as you. You will find these people to be the easiest to start a conversation with. You already have something in common with them, so the start of your conversation is easier.

I belonged to a gym for seven years and never understood why I could not meet anyone there. I worked out on the machines, smiled at people and was friendly. Then, one day, I decided to take a yoga class at the gym. It was filled with other people who also liked yoga. I instantly had something to talk about with them and started making new friends within weeks. See also "Influence—How to Create It, How to Keep It" by Caterina Rando on page 93.

## Where Do You Want to Meet Them?

Meeting strangers can be stressful for most people. Why not make it easy on yourself by already knowing something about the person you are approaching? Did you join a kayaking group? That's great! You already know the person you are approaching likes to kayak or they would not be there.

It is easy to use Google® with your zip code, a hobby you like, and groups or meetups. For instance, if you live within the zip code 94521, and you like to sew, you can use Google to search 94521, sewing, groups and find others who like to sew or stores who sell sewing supplies. This is a great start to meeting new people! You will find "S.E.W.," which is a series of workshops for people who sew! How easy was that?

The more specific you are about the interest you have, the more you will have to talk about with the people you will meet. I can go to a wine tasting because I like wine, or I can go to the "Pinot Wine Tasting" and know that everyone there is interested in or loves Pinot. This gives me an instant "in" with almost every person there because I love Pinot specifically and so do they!

# Whom Do You Want to Meet?

When you go to an event by yourself, who exactly do you want to meet? Well frankly, you are nervous and just want someone who will be nice to you. Even though your mouth is dry, your stomach is shaky or you feel like you are blushing, do not just run up to the first person you see and start talking. Being pushy is just as offensive as snubbing people is. Be more selective with the people you approach.

You want to meet people who are just as interested in talking to you as you are with them. You will be able to sense this as you walk through the room, and you will approach those people. Seek out people who feel comfortable, or are familiar to you. Perhaps they have shoes, a handbag or a jacket that you really like. Perhaps they will be sipping on a cocktail that you are about to order. The last event I went to was in a room of seventy-five people with whom I had no connection. I was very nervous when I came in. I tried to approach two different women who were not very responsive to me. I looked across the room and saw a woman who was holding a book I had just bought. That was enough for me to approach her and start my first conversation.

# Whom Do You Talk To?

You may think that because I am a socializing expert, it is easy for me to go to events by myself and make new friends. However, it is not always easy for me, and my expertise comes from years and years of forcing myself to overcome the shyness that ensues when you are in a room filled with people you do not know.

Entering the room can be a bit intimidating when people are standing around talking to one another. I usually find a table that has brochures on it, business cards or some sort of literature. This gives you the opportunity to look like you are busy while you are getting yourself together to talk to your first person. After your initial nerves have settled, start walking. Observe anyone who is making eye contact with you even for a brief second. Are they also by themselves? Is there a group of more than three people you can approach? If there are several groups of people, which groups seems the most animated?

The best way to begin your socializing is to just smile and walk up to someone. Regardless of whether you have chosen one person to approach or a group, please remember to smile. You do not have to have a cheek-to-cheek grin. Just turn up the corners of your mouth.

## What Is the Best Way to Approach a New Person?

Most people like compliments. Here we are at an event. We have gotten all dressed up, our hair looks good, I personally just got my eyebrows waxed, and I've checked my makeup a few times. Wouldn't it make sense that we feel happy when someone notices our hard work?

If I am going to approach someone new, I will find something about him or her that I like. "I really love your shoes, where did you get them?" or "I love your bag, and I haven't been able to find one like that." Usually, this person will respond with where they got it or will thank you for the compliment. This is your chance to start a conversation.

You have other options aside from making a compliment. You can start by smiling and saying, "Hi, I'm [insert your name]. This is my first time here. Are you a member?" All you need is one good introduction line, and then you can start small talk. Small talk is the first level of contact with a person before you can move on to deeper levels of connection with them.

The wonderful thing about small talk is this: It is the start of any relationship you will have with another person. Because you engage in it every day, it should feel very natural for you. The grocery store, the gas station and most retail stores are small talk utopia! "How are you?" "Enjoying the weather?" and "Did you see the game?" are all examples of common small talk. This can easily be translated into a happy hour conversation, "How's it going?" "What are you drinking?" and "What do you do for a living?" These questions all help you gauge if the person you are talking to is responsive to you and whether you can take your conversation further.

## How to Follow Up

Assuming that the conversation will go fantastic, and you will spend a good fifteen minutes with this person engaged in conversation, there will be a time when you will need to move on to another person. You can leave the conversation with the intent on talking to this person again by saying, "Do you have a business card on you?" or "Are you on Facebook®, LinkedIn®?" This is your segue into re-connecting with this person. By email, friending on Facebook or connecting on LinkedIn, you can stay in touch and find out when the next meeting, event or networking opportunity is.

## Start Meeting, Mixing and Making the Most of Your Connections

Being able to socialize with people is essential. Most of the education in your life has come from other people. Whether you went to a baseball game, shopped at a mall or went to a family reunion, you learned something from someone every place you went. Interaction with the people around you is the essence of life! You have the biggest Wikipedia® ever—the people around you! Asking questions and exchanging thoughts and opinions with others makes your life more interesting. The knowledge you will gain from this has endless possibilities.

Knowledge is just the beginning. As in my ladder story, making social ties with others helps you accomplish greater tasks than you can on your own and with greater speed and efficiency. None of my Facebook friends could have jumped off my iPhone®—which was locked in my apartment—and helped me. Nothing can substitute human interaction and the benefit of new friends.

*"Basic human contact - the meeting of eyes, the exchanging of words - is to the psyche what oxygen is to the brain. If you're feeling abandoned by the world, interact with anyone you can."*
—Martha Beck, American sociologist and author

Choose an event to attend in the next week or two and practice making small talk with strangers. Before long, those strangers will be your friends!

RACHEL ESTELLE
Meet, Mix and Make the Most
of Your Connections

(415) 516-3755
SocialMixology@gmail.com
www.SocialMixology101.com

*S*OCIAL MIXOLOGIST and speaker Rachel Estelle believes the key to your success is how you interact with people. Your client relationships, business networking opportunities and marketing goals are all dependent on how well you mingle with others.

Rachel brings more than twenty years of experience in client interaction, including nine years in the salon and spa industry. She has had a diverse career path that has included customer service in property management, reception, sales, leasing, retail, salon management and human resources. She has always been motivated by her fascination for human behavior and social interaction. Her ability to work with a variety of personalities was honed in the real world and is unparalleled.

Rachel coaches small business owners, entrepreneurs and other professionals who want to increase their self-confidence in social situations. Whether it is improving presentation skills, overcoming networking shyness, or dealing with difficult clients, every situation is an opportunity to improve your social skills. Rachel's programs include "Mixing Confidence with Your Career Change," "Putting the Fizz in your Business with Social Media," "Turning Your Clients into Regulars," and "Sales with a Twist."

# Styleguru *Mantra* for Solutions Inherent in You

by Pankaj Sabharwal

O N A SUNDAY evening, I got a distress call from Mark and Rita, whom I had met at a friend's party. Both were very upset because Rita had gotten a layoff notice at her workplace. The reason given was that her personal style did not match the image of the company.

I met them at their house the next morning and wore a lively printed shirt with jeans and loafers since I wanted to project a relaxed and cheerful image. The stress was evident from Rita's face. She wore a shoulder-padded, long tee shirt with tights in a style of the 1980s. Her shoulders were as wide as her hips, and her waist was narrow. She had a figure-eight shape.

After talking to Rita, I realized that she was very knowledgeable and innocent at heart. She was beautiful both inside and out and had a pure soul. However, she had lost her confidence and was stressed, not because of losing her job, but because she had been "branded" as "old-fashioned"and not fitting the image of the company.

We are all born in this life with an innocent heart. The idea of an "innocent" or "pure" heart is one that is God-fearing and loves others as opposed to only self-love. Truly achieving and becoming beautiful inside and out means that personal appearance must go hand-in-hand with values as a subtext to the soul's desires and the spirit's intent. Once we learn to be true to ourselves and be good to others, we have a heart that is pure and fulfills the purpose of creation.

> *"He/She who is busy doing good finds no time to look good."*
> —Rabindranath Tagore, Indian Nobel Prize® laureate,
> author and musician

## Styleguru Mantra—Meditation and Style Correction

Mantras originated in Vedic traditions of India. They are a single word or group of words that have the power of complete transformation. The primordial mantra *Om* is said to be the original sound that was present at the creation of the universe. It is said to be the primary sound that contains all other sounds, all words, all languages and all mantras.

A mantra is a particular sound or vibration repeated silently in your mind. It takes you to an expanding awareness, enhances and balances the process and provides a greater reality, which is the real source of everything we experience. The objective of these forms of meditative practices is to open the mind into a comprehensive awareness of everything happening without a distinctive focus. The capacity to be present with whatever arises is developed through this practice.

Scientific research from *The IONS Meditation Bibliography* shows that meditation slows your breathing, decreases blood pressure and lowers your stress hormone levels. *The IONS Meditation Bibliography* is the largest and most comprehensive known catalogue of published scientific studies of meditation in the world. IONS maintains this database and updates it quarterly with current research. *The IONS Meditation Bibliography* was originally compiled and edited by Michael Murphy, cofounder of Esalen Institute, in collaboration with

Steven Donovan. It was published in print in 1997 as *"The Physical and Psychological Effects of Meditation: a Review of Contemporary Research."*

I had both Mark and Rita meditate and chant Mantra Om with closed eyes. After a few minutes of this meditating practice, the couple started looking and feeling better with increased feelings of vitality and rejuvenation. It helped in resolving their phobias and fears, further making them experience an inner sense of assurance.

Now, it was time for Rita's style evolution—she needed a serious makeover. Her wardrobe *was* from the eighties. She had acid-wash jeans denim jackets, shoulder-padded dresses and chunky jewelry, and the colors she wore were bright. As a mother of two teenagers, she needed to shed her eighties image and enter into the elegance of her age and figure type. Since she was smart and knowledgeable, it took no time to move toward achieving her desired transformation.

As a figure eight silhouette, Rita needed belted garments, straight skirts and flared or straight pants. Unstructured jackets with curved lines and a defined waist without shoulder pads also looked good on her. We tossed her acid-wash jeans, denim jackets and chunky jewelry. Then, we took clothing that could be altered, removed the shoulder pads from them, toned down the colors and added accessories, such as handbags, scarves, beaded and semi-precious jewelry.

Rita's knowledge, experience, patience and new style got her a better job in a bigger corporation. The couple came out of stress, frustration and low self-esteem. They started believing in themselves, accepted compliments graciously and improved business and social interactions.

A peaceful mind and corrective dressing techniques can give you confidence and make a difference in your life and career. Understanding your body shape is essential for a stylish appearance and for making a good first impression. This will free you to express yourself better, win hearts, make friends and influence others. Clothes have a magical power to accentuate the positive and eliminate the negative aspects of your body. Therefore, recognizing your body shape and being confident is the first vital step of transformation to a successful you. Remember, confidence is not something you show when you are successful. Confidence is something you show after consistent failures!

# Defining Your Shape, Assessing Your Figure

Your shoulder, waist and hips determine your natural silhouette.

- **Rectangular figure shape.** Shoulders are as wide as the hips, the waist is not defined or is a little narrower than shoulder or hips and gives a rectangular look.

  **Tip:** The waist of garments, such as shirts, pants, skirts, dresses and jackets needs to be defined or given a little emphasis with accessories.

- **Oval figure shape.** The shoulder and hips are relatively smaller than the waist, and from the front, the waist appears noticeably wider.

  **Tip:** Balance by widening the shoulders and not defining the waist. Do not wear double-breasted or structured jackets.

- **Triangle figure type.** The hips and thighs are wider than the shoulders, and the waist is relatively high.

  **Tip:** Extend the shoulders to balance the wider part of hips and thighs and wear shoulder pads or structured jackets.

- **Figure eight shape.** The shoulder and hips are wide and curved, and the waist is distinctly narrow.

  **Tip:** Wear straight pants and skirts and dresses with princess seam lines. Avoid shoulder pads.

- **Hourglass figure shape.** The shoulders are straight and as wide as the hips, the waist is not broad or wide and looks like an hourglass.

  **Tip:** Create lines from shoulder to hem, and choose raglan sleeves.

- **Inverted triangle figure type.** The shoulders are wider than the hips, and the waist is narrow.

  **Tip:** Wear A-line dresses or dresses that make the lower body appear as wide as the shoulders. Flared or straight-legged pants are a good option.

# Be Open to Grace

I like the expression of "opening to grace" from Marianne Williamson's book *A Return to Love,* published by Harper Paperbacks in 1996. She writes, "To open to grace is to ask that only loving, helpful thoughts remain in our minds, and all the rest be let go."

When there are no impurities in your mind, you are pure and honest to yourself, and this leads to the principle "Open to Grace." You become inherently pure. The natural state of mind is pure and radiant. When we open to the wisdom within, the truth of our emotions often opens to the abundance of knowledge, which is within all of us. By embracing good, de-cluttering your mind and discovering the power and consciousness beyond the ego, you achieve inherent purity and feel satisfied at having achieved your desires. Grace is the force that lives within you and guides you to make the right decisions.

In simple words of Max Storm in his book *A Life Worth Breathing: A Yoga Master's Handbook of Strength, Grace, and Healing,* published by Skyhorse Publishing in 2010, "When we meditate or pray, we reach out towards God. Grace is when God reaches back to us."

Meditation gives you the power to become stronger at transforming into a pure soul and prepares you to face the hectic lifestyle by rejuvenating your spirits. Listen to your emotions, and they will give you the answers you need.

Using the principle *Open to Grace* helps decision making. For example, most of my clients understand their body type and corrective dressing options. However, they often cannot decide if a combination would look good. They need the power to be decisive. This can be achieved by inherent purity, which would lead their emotions to give them the answer. Your appearance, behavior and communication become naturally beautiful and confident, and you project a magnetic aura.

## Fashion Fads vs. Body Types

A fashion fad is a fashion that is taken up with great enthusiasm for a brief period of time. It is an interest followed with exaggerated zeal. Please do not blindly follow the fashion fads, know your body first.

> *"They know they are going to look beautiful,*
> *and I don't think women should look like costumes.*
> *They shouldn't look like fashion victims."*
> —Ralph Lauren, American fashion designer

The Styleguru Mantra is, "Opt for styles that suit, rather than styles that are in vogue, as the styles that suit automatically become a rage and come in vogue."

Approach these fads with caution and keep your body shape in mind.

- Leggings have been a fad since 2010 and are appropriate only for people with lean legs.

- Harem pants can be worn as loungewear.

- Flip-flops are considered comfortable and can be worn appropriately with casual clothing.

- Bohemian fashion is a casual mix of hippie, ethnic, gypsy and vintage elements. It is not only a fashion fad. It also is a state of mind that reflects a lifestyle that seemingly dismisses fashion. No one can afford to wear bohemian fashion to work or a business meeting.

- Oversize glasses were in fashion in the seventies and have made a comeback. They are best worn as infrequent accessories to match a particular style.

Marcella was an artist and was working in college as an art teacher. She was so much into her art that she almost forgot about herself, her family and friends. She was single, in her early thirties and had no interest in shopping, eating out or movies. Her mother, Martha, was my client and wanted my help to give Marcella direction and upgrade her image. Since Marcella appeared to be at least twenty years older than she actually was, her mother was afraid that her appearance hindered Marcella from forming relationships with men.

Martha wanted me to transform not only her daughter's appearance, but also her nature or character. I took this as a challenge and went to Marcella's painting exhibition at a nearby gallery. She wore a beige, A-line skirt with a green printed loose-fitting shirt, no makeup and messy hair. However, her beautiful eyes and forehead revealed innocence. Her paintings were extraordinary. When you looked at them, you felt as if they were talking to you.

In one painting, a woman was meditating with the rising sun as a background. After I showed interest in buying that painting, Marcella opened up to me, and we started talking about the inspiration behind that painting. She revealed how much she wanted to meditate, but she was so much engrossed in her work that she had no time for that.

We made an instant connection and decided to meditate together. We started meditating exercises every morning, and it gradually led us to *opening to grace.* The breathing exercises led us to longer gaps between inhalation and exhalation, and we started enjoying the long pauses as if we were in a state of not breathing. The focus on the breath enabled us to let go of any thoughts we had and relax our mind and body, so it could rejuvenate and heal. It gave us peace of mind, happiness and helped us discover purpose.

Improving your self-image through understanding the psychology of mind and soul and having a more positive attitude can open you to a world of physical changes. In addition to changing your way of thinking, you can also change your behavior and abilities by learning new skills.

This brought such a huge difference in Marcella's life that she decided to seek my help. Together we made a to-do list, in which appearance was one of the subjects she wanted attention on.

Being a painter, Marcella knew the importance of color and was more than willing to introduce coloring in her styles. We went on a shopping trip and bought the right clothes for her figure type. We achieved a new look and a new person. Marcella had been hidiing inside. Her smile was genuine, and her charm had a magnetic aura.

> *"You must find the place inside yourself where*
> *nothing is impossible."*
> —Deepak Chopra, Indian author

Whatever you want to achieve, you can have it—just never give up on what you really want to do. The person with big dreams is more powerful than the one with just the facts. The information you acquire will create a lifelong understanding of how to use style to add to your personal power.

Styleguru Mantra helps you understand how to exude confidence, power and presence. The way you look affects your attitude, and confidence creates a presence when you walk into a room. You and your wardrobe will send a message of being in control.

Meditation will give you a pure mind, and honesty will lead to the principle Open to Grace. You play a huge part in your happiness, and you can greatly increase it by taking action and changing your attitude toward yourself. Your true emotions will always give you the right answers whenever you get lost in multiple options. Your body, mind and spirit get in harmony, and you learn the art of forgiveness. Always remember, you are responsible for yourself, and your happiness depends upon what you tell yourself, how you treat yourself and how you interpret your world. Believe in yourself and believe that you are capable of handling life's problems.

*"Beauty is how you feel inside, and it reflects in your eyes.*
*It is not something physical."*
—Sophia Loren, Italian film actress

I don't know if success gives you happiness, but I know a pure mind and a smiling face can lead you to success. Fearlessness is not something one is born with—it is something each one of us has to walk into. With inner strength and confidence, your aura will become magnetic, and the strength of your eye contact will be unbelievable.

PANKAJ SABHARWAL
Founder and President
Styleguru Fashion Hub

*Be Yourself, Be at Ease*

(416) 907-9641
pankaj@style-guru.com
www.style-guru.com
www.stylegurumantra.com

PANKAJ SABHARWAL, known as "*Styleguru*," is the founder and president of *Styleguru Fashion Hub*, and began his journey in India as a fashion designer and stylist. As a trained fashion designer, Pankaj designs both couture and *prêt a porter* for men and women. He has styled looks for numerous models, celebrities and Bollywood film stars. Fashion critics appreciate his creativity, craftsmanship and talent. His collections have received rave reviews from print and electronic media.

In his fifteen years of experience, Pankaj has taken the measurements of more than 3,000 clients and customized clothes for them. This has helped him become the master of body analysis and of camouflaging figure variation with perfectly tailored clothing. Pankaj helps his clients in eliminating impulse buying, refine their shopping skills and increasing their wardrobe visibility.

An international image consultant, Pankaj started *style-guru.com* as a complete solution for your styling, color, shopping, wardrobe and makeover challenges. His aim is to transform an average body into a masterpiece of perfection and design by focusing on assets and concealing shape challenges.

# $\mathscr{Influence}$—How to Get It, How to Keep It

by Caterina Rando, MA, MCC

THE SOCIALLY smart and savvy person knows that being well known, being popular or being recognized does not mean you have influence. After all, what good is it to have everyone know your name and your face if they do not know what you do, or how respected you are in your field, or how smart or reliable you are? What is far worse is if everyone knows you and seeks to avoid you when they see you because you never stop talking about yourself, or no one recommends or refers others to you because you have a reputation for being rude?

Influence is the ability to affect others, to impact their thoughts and actions toward your desired outcome. Influence equals ease in creating what you want in your professional and personal life. Cultivating influence with the people in your network is really where your attention will reap the most reward. What matters is who trusts you, respects you, remembers you, has a deep understanding of what you do or the contribution you make and wants to help you. When you can create all this with one of your contacts, you now have influence. Influence and being socially smart and savvy go hand in hand—your ability to influence others is a key component of how effective you can become.

Without influence, whatever you are doing that involves other people is harder—getting clients is harder, getting people to listen to you is harder, and even getting your phone calls returned is harder. Everything is harder without influence.

I want you to enjoy a life where exciting opportunities come to you regularly, where every time you walk into a room—a boardroom, a ballroom or your local coffee shop—people know your name and are thrilled to see you. I want you to have a life where you get through to other influential people when you call them, where all your invitations are accepted and your friends, clients and charity project colleagues say a resounding yes to working with you even before they meet you. That is the kind of life influential people enjoy every day and that is what I want for you. Here is my equation for building influence, and I encourage you to embrace it immediately.

## Visibility + Value + Consistency = Influence

Visibility is simply showing up online and offline. A product brand has to be seen several times by someone before they will purchase a product. The same is sometimes true for building influence with the people in your network. When people see you in a variety of places and situations, you have different opportunities to connect—this builds influence. How can you be more visible and therefore more influential today? A few ideas are, you can become the head of a charity committee, be sure to go to all the social events you are invited to, or host your own social event to bring people together.

Value occurs when you give, share or assist someone with something that they find useful. You can let them know about a resource that can save their company money, tell them about a book you think they will enjoy, or have an authentic conversation where they feel really seen and heard by you. These are just a few examples of providing value. Where can you provide value to people in your network that also enhances your influence?

Consistency of good behavior is key for building influence with others. This includes consistently being on time, meeting deadlines, being responsive and being open and receptive to ideas. Are you consistent in your professional life? Where could you improve consistency and, thus, influence?

Remember the Visibility + Value + Consistency = Influence equation as you read the rest of this chapter. This is the foundation of your plan to cultivate influence.

Sometimes, influence is bestowed simply because of position, as is the case with a company CEO or elected official. Many people bestow influence on the wealthy or "the beautiful people." This kind of influence is outside of what I will focus on here. Follow the strategies in this chapter to create more influence starting today, in whatever position you hold, with whatever economic level you enjoy in whatever social circles you move in. These ideas will build your influence with everyone you already know and everyone you will meet in the future. You can use them to become socially savvy.

## Be Positive

A smile looks good on everyone. It conveys welcome and says, "I am happy to talk with you." It is the easiest way to be friendly and approachable.

When you have a positive disposition, people are much more likely to connect with you. Here is something you probably know from psychology that absolutely applies to building influence. The biggest predictor of future behavior is past behavior. If the last time someone met you on an elevator or saw you at an event, you were complaining about something, he or she would be less likely to reach out to you again because the last impression of you was negative. Your past behavior will influence other's ideas about your future behavior.

Be positive, do not complain and do not criticize yourself or others. If a smile makes everyone more beautiful, a complaint or gossip makes everyone ugly. People want to associate with, invite and recommend people whom they want to be around.

## Demonstrate a Genuine Interest in Others

Early in my career, I attended a business event with one of my mentors. I was impressed when she walked up to people she did not know, smiled, put out her hand and said, "Hi, I am Kimberly. I have not met you yet."

Everyone she approached responded with a smile and a handshake. They gave her their names and conversation ensued. I use this everywhere. I follow up the introductions by asking a couple of interested, open-ended questions about the person. My favorite question is to ask them what is the newest or most exciting thing going on with them or what is the best thing that has happened to them lately. People love to answer these questions because it gives them an opportunity to shine and lets them talk about whatever they like.

People will find you charming, smart and interesting—even if you hardly say anything. This is what I call influence with ease.

Once you have met someone, you have to get to know him or her and if your first interaction was a positive one, you begin to build trust. Build on that first meeting by doing a few simple things. Remember someone's name, friend them on Facebook® or LinkedIn® right away, so you will have their picture. Immediately follow up on any action you agreed to take. Send a nice-to-meet-you note—it is done so rarely these days, and definitely serves to build influence for you and makes a great follow-up to a strong first impression.

# Have a Strong Personal Brand

Your behavior, your presence, your personality and your professional image have to be consistent in order to convey the impression you want to make. Your personal brand is not just the colors you use in your personal stationary. Your appearance, your behavior and your communication are all part of your personal brand. You may have had your colors done, worked with an image professional and have a great smile that makes you approachable. None of this matters if you show up only fifty percent of the time to a committee meeting, are always late and never offer to help. The people on the committee will perceive you as unreliable at best, flaky at worst, and you will have no influence with any of them.

Give attention to your personal brand. One of my favorite personal branding exercises as it relates to influence is to write down six or seven words that you want people to say about you. Put those words in front of you in your home or office and read them every day. Make sure everything you say and do, and everything that represents you, such as a website, receptionist or voicemail message, reflects these words. For example, the words I have posted in front of me in my office are "honest, positive, warm, approachable, generous, dynamic and excellent." I make sure everything that happens in my life and business reflects these words. I make it easy for people to connect with me, and my team and I are always striving for better client care and better responsiveness personally.

## Cultivate Community, Connection and Camaraderie

You have influence with people who know you, trust you, like you and think highly of you and or your skills. It can sometimes be impossible to meet and get to know the people with whom you want to cultivate influence. You can overcome this challenge by consciously implementing your fun, social and professional community-building plans. Ask yourself what you can do to consistently and effectively build your relationships and cultivate camaraderie in all areas of your life. Here are some ideas to get you started.

**Invite people to go where you are going.** This is a great way to let people know that you want to get to know them better. Whenever you are going to a conference, a seminar, a charity luncheon or even a yoga class, think about whom you want to get to know better who would appreciate an invitation. Invite several people to join you at once, and they will start by telling each other how wonderful you are. This definitely helps with influence building.

**Host personal events.** Many influential people hold an annual backyard barbeque or a holiday event, or put together a group to participate in a walkathon followed by a party. Note, I said, "annual event." Consistency over time creates results. One event is good, and a strategy of consistently hosting events is far better.

**Host online business and professional events.** A few years ago, I developed a new niche with image consultants for my business consulting and training practice. In order to get "in front" of as many image professionals as possible, I started to host free, information-packed tele-classes. This brought me clients from four continents that I have never met and built my reputation as a business-building expert in that industry. This is an easy way to cultivate influence. Hosting webinars is equally effective.

**Host offline business and professional events.** There is nothing better than inviting potential clients and people in your field to your own events. This could be an evening workshop or a reception to celebrate the release of your new book, an anniversary reception or an open house. Any reason to invite people to be with you at an event you are hosting is a great idea. In most cases, you have more influence with people after you have met them in person. See also "Entertaining and Being the Gracious Host" by Sharon Ringiér on page 163.

**Start your own large or small association or group.** When you are the founder and leader of a group, you receive some "insta-influence." If you want to be a part of a group of professionals that learn about building wealth—start one. If you want to get to know people who are in the same industry as you in your city—start a group. Start a mastermind group, or start a group of people who raise money for a charitable cause you care about. This is a great way to build your network, hone your leadership skills and, of course, create influence. Return emails and phone calls promptly. I know this is tough with super busy lives, and it is more important than ever. Because the people in your network know you receive a lot of calls and emails, you make a greater impression when you get right back to people. It shows you care.

**Connect in online communities.** Reach out on a daily or weekly basis to people you want to meet or whom you already know and have not yet connected with online. Sometimes, when I travel to another city for business, I invite my Facebook friends and LinkedIn connections to join me for a networking reception. This is a great way to make your online connections count. These receptions have resulted in new clients and opportunities.

# Be Generous

Being generous feels great. I know this first-hand because my mother has always been a happy, generous person. She was an elementary school teacher for many years, and she often stayed late to work with students who needed extra help. She gave supplies to children who could not afford them and always greeted both students and teachers by name and with a smile. She was the most influential teacher in her school without even trying.

There is an Italian saying she used as a guiding principle in life that I want you to embrace: *Fa bene, e disricordare,* which translates into "do good and forget about it."

I was shocked recently when I heard a celebrity say she keeps track of all the kind things she does for someone, so she can remind them of it when she needs something. This is ridiculous. Do good and forget about it. The law of reciprocity will keep track for you.

There are five unique ways to be generous, five different ways to show someone you genuinely care about them and want to help. You can give them your time, your money, words of appreciation or encouragement, gifts and your contacts. Be generous with all of these. Pick up the check, buy the fundraising candy bar, accept the invitation for coffee someone extends to ask your advice. Do everything you can to connect people with the people they want to meet.

When thinking about being generous with your time, this can also mean being generous with your listening or being generous with advice or guidance. Another way to be generous is to invite and include people in a meeting or event you think would benefit them. I often invite people as my guests to my live trainings because I know they will get value from it. This creates goodwill and cultivates great relationships.

Another favorite thing I do is invite people to go where I am going. This combines one idea from above with being generous. If I am going to a luncheon, a networking event or a workshop, I invite several people whom I know would enjoy attending. Creating influence is magnified when you have a table full of people who all know you and do not yet know each other. The first thing they do is talk about you and how fabulous you are!

## Communicating Your Needs

Once you have strong rapport with people, make requests of them for business or contacts. If you ask people to hire you as soon as they meet you, you will probably see hesitation on their part and sometimes even resentment. It is naive to expect people to use your services or refer others to you until you have created influence. See also "Savvy Interaction" by Katrina Van Dopp on page 37.

Influence is cultivated over time. Look at the people in your network. Have you created good rapport with them? Do you stay in regular contact so they remember you? Are you generous? If so, it is time to think about how you can use your influence to grow your business by asking people to refer others to work with you. If not, get working on what you have learned here. The more influence you have, the more your business will thrive, and the more what you want will come to you with ease.

**CATERINA RANDO,** MA, MCC
**Business Strategist, Speaker, Publisher**

*Solutions to Make You Thrive*

(415) 668-4535
cat@caterinarando.com
www.caterinarando.com
www.caterinaspeaks.com
www.thrivebooks.com

CATERINA RANDO'S mission is to show women how to be loud and proud about who they are and the value they bring. She is a sought-after speaker, business strategist and author of the national bestseller, *Learn to Power Think* from Chronicle Books. She is featured as a success expert in several leading business books including *Savvy Leadership Strategies for Woman, Entrepreneur Extraordinaire, Incredible Business* and *Make Your Connections Count.*

Since 1993, Caterina has been providing consulting, training and solutions to ensure women entrepreneurs succeed. Through her Business Breakthrough Summit, Sought After Speaker Summit and Luxury Retreat for Women Entrepreneurs, she and her team show women how to become recognized as experts, think and plan strategically and significantly grow their revenue.

Caterina is also the founder of THRIVE Publishing™, a company that publishes books, including this book, for experts who want to share their message with a greater market. She holds a bachelor of science degree in organizational behavior and a master of arts degree in life transitions counseling psychology. She is a certified personal and professional coach (CPPC) and a master certified coach (MCC), the highest designation awarded by the International Coaching Federation™.

# The *Language* of Shopping

by Shai Thompson

WE ALL know someone who always looks put together, who emanates an aura of self-assurance that seems so effortless. They give off an essence of authentic power, taste and knowledge. People who are successful in work, relationships and presentation have a special something. They have taken to heart and answered the question: What do I want and what do I need?

The answer gives you the language to declare your needs and have them met.

Your beauty is like a diamond, multidimensional with many facets. For success to occur, it is vital that you understand your facets—your likes and dislikes—to connect your internal identity with your external image. This is your style declaration.

*"Our deepest fear is not that we are inadequate. Our deepest fear is that we are powerful beyond measure. It is our light, not our darkness that most frightens us. We ask ourselves, who am I to be brilliant, gorgeous, talented and fabulous?*
*Actually, who are you not to be?"*
—Marianne Williamson, American author

Change is painful for most. Think of the caterpillar, which changes into a butterfly. Now, this is an amazing achievement! Just like a butterfly, you can change into a unique expression of yourself by making the commitment. I realize it sounds so simple, yet it is not—it takes work. Just like life, your style will forever be in transition. With each transition, you will find it easier to make the adjustment by learning these skills of style declaration.

I have designed a formula very much like a business plan to help you. There are a vision statement, mission statement, budget, action plan, and an assessment of strengths, weakness, opportunities and threats. Using my formula will create a look that manifests the essence of your authentic presentation and is uniquely you.

When defining the outward projection of yourself, you must first look inward to identify who you are. Ultimately, your guidance comes from your inner identity connecting with your external image.

**Identity + Image + Internal + External = Projection of personal style**

You will make nine declarations, one for each of the following areas:

1. Lifestyle
2. Activities
3. Fabric and color
4. Shopping habits
5. Age-appropriate style
6. Style type
7. The look you want
8. Figure analysis
9. Color analysis

With each declaration, write a concise sentence that makes the description clear. After you have written the nine declarations, arrange them all into a paragraph. This is your declaration summary. From this, you will have the power of your own language to describe clearly your wants and needs. Here is an example:

*My name is Betty Dewitt, a 28-year-old office manager with an active social calendar. Unmarried, no children, gives me the freedom to travel one to two times per year and to date actively. My shopping and dressing habits have led me to a frustrated, I-give-up mentality. I hate shopping. I never go. As a result, I am not looking as good as I could. I never do a seasonal change in my closet—the term is alien to me as is consignment shopping and online shopping. I do know what "put together" looks like. I just can't seem to do it for myself.*

*I have always loved Reese Witherspoon's sense of style. I love linen and cotton for spring and summer and cashmere and wool for fall and winter. Typically dark for winter—black, brown and navy and for spring and summer, I am white, gray, black. I do not like synthetic fabrics or patterns of any kind. I am a machine-wash-hang-to-dry kind of girl. My body shape is hourglass, and I am a winter.*

**Lifestyle declaration.** Lifestyle is your way of living on a day-to-day basis. What you do at work or at play? What are your daily interests, friends, family? What are your values, needs, wants and attitude? What is your social class, income, culture? Do you travel? Declare your lifestyle in one or two sentences.

**Example:** My name is Betty, and I am a 28-year-old office manager with an active social calendar. Unmarried, no children gives me the freedom to actively date and travel. I am spiritually guided and love the company of like-minded family and friends.

**Activities declaration.** Activities you may engage in daily. Working out, gardening, reading, cooking, shopping. Do your activities change seasonally? Do you volunteer?

**Example:** I walk to work every day of the year and love cooking and gardening when I get home. Yoga three times a week year round and in the winter, I like to cross country ski.

**Fabrics and colors declaration.** Knowing what fabrics and colors you like and dislike. What patterns do you like and dislike? What are your favorite colors to wear in each season? Are you a summer, spring, winter or fall?

**Example:** I love linen and cotton for spring and summer and cashmere and wool for fall and winter. Typically dark for winter, black, brown, navy, and white, grey, blue-black for spring and summer. I do not like synthetic fabrics or patterns of any kind. I am a winter.

**Shopping habits declaration.** What kind of a shopper are you? Habits. Are you a mall or a boutique shopper? Do you shop online? Do you tend to buy one item at a time or do you buy the entire outfit? Do you like to shop? Do you shop in consignment stores? Do you make and follow through with a budget?

**Example:** My shopping and dressing habits have led me into a "frustrated, I-give-up" situation. I hate shopping. I never go. As a result, I am not looking as good as I could. The term "consignment shopping" is alien to me. Who would want what I have?

**Age-appropriate style declaration.** Here are some guidelines:

• **Twenties:** Stay out of your mother's closet. Stay away from matronly looking clothes. Anything goes. Appreciate the tone and shape you have now. Try different styles, experiment with accessories. Plunging neck and back lines and miniskirts are a go!

- **Thirties:** Investment pieces show off your sophisticated taste. Choose quality fabrics. Find a tailor. It is time to enjoy living in the "you-can-wear-anything" age. Embrace sexy!

- **Forties:** Stay out of your daughter's closet. Great time to invest in a classic suit that transitions from corporate to cocktail. Keep a sleek, no-frills rule combined with trendy accessories. Aim for classic and edgy.

- **Fifties:** Express yourself with impact accessories and monochromatic fabrics that layer well. As you age, your skin tone changes along with the texture of our hair. To find your new colors that compliment you, have a color analysis from an expert.

- **Sixties:** The self-assured wisdom of your beauty keeps you aware of fashion trends, modern cuts and skin-flattering tones. If your arms are toned, show them off. If not, cover up with a chic wrap.

- **Seventies:** Do not buy a purple and red hat. Judy Dench is an ageless woman who wears classic, chic pieces—follow her lead.

- **Eighties:** Do whatever you want. You have earned it.

**Style Type declaration.** Which one of these best describes you? You can choose more than one. By assessing your style type, you can determine your clothing personality that further defines your overall style. You will save time and money by choosing style-type appropriate items for your wardrobe.

- **Classic:** Simple, easy to wear, clean lines, not into fads, traditional, recognizes and values standard of excellence.

- **Chic:** Hip, dramatic, sophisticated, fashionable lifestyle, wearing the latest and popular, high quality.

- **Whimsical:** Artistic, romantic, unpredictable.

- **Bohemian:** Ethnic, unconventional, hippie-like, loose fit, oversized, tunics, peace love.

- **Natural:** Folk, country, jeans and tee's, very casual.

- **Avant Garde:** Intellectual, experimental, dark, Goth, independent.

- **Sporty:** Yoga wear, active wear, outdoors.

**Example:** I am a combination of three style types. I would say I enjoy classic foundation items accessorized by dramatic chic pieces while staying natural.

**Your shopping list.** Your time is valuable and if you plan well, you will shop wisely. Essentials are the foundation pieces of your wardrobe. For example, a black suit for a business woman is a versatile essential. A non-essential item is a pair of red stilettos that takes the black essential suit from corporate to cocktail.

The following are general suggestions created to complete a seasonal essential/non-essential wardrobe. After you have purchased the item, make sure to check it off.

### Spring and Summer Shopping List

| | | |
|---|---|---|
| • 2 Versatile sundresses | • 2 Skirts | • 1 Lightweight work tote |
| | • 1 Denim skirt | |
| • 4 T-shirts in neutrals | | • 2 Shopping totes |
| • 4 Cotton tank + camisole | • 1 Trench coat | • 1 Structured handbag |
| • 2 Short sleeve blouse | • 1 Day wrap | • 1 Evening clutch |
| | • 1 Evening wrap | |
| • 2 White jeans + khakis | | • 2 Swimsuits |
| • 2 Shorts: 1 dressy, 1 casual | • 1 Fashion sneakers | • 1 Swimsuit cover up |
| | • 2 Flat sandals | |
| • 1 Feminine, fitted blazer | • 1 Espadrilles | • 2 Summer hats |
| • 1 Short casual jacket | • 2 Open toe/sling back heel | |
| • 2 Lightweight cardigan | | |

## Fall and Winter Shopping List

- 2 Little black dress
- 1 Jersey silk wrap dress

- 2 Turtlenecks, V-necks or crew necks
- 2 Cardigans
- 2 Wrap cardigans

- 2 White shirts
- 1 Silk blouse
- 1 Dark shirt

- 1 Boot-cut black pant
- 1 Straight leg black pant
- 1 Wool trousers
- 1 Corduroy pant
- 1 Dressy and 1 casual jean

- A-line or kick pleat skirt
- Pencil or straight skirt

- 2 Blazers
- 1 Wool pant suit

- 1 Long winter coat
- 1 Weekend wear jacket

- 2 Black pump
- 1 Kitten heel
- 1 Flat shoes
- 2 Boots

- 1 Work tote
- 1 Structured handbag

**Figure analysis.** There are three vertical body types:

- The balanced body is equal distance from the top of head to hip and hip to toe.
- The long-leg short body is most common with tall women and some short women.
- The short-leg long body is usually short to average height.

**Example:** I have a balanced body with equal distance from the top of my head to hip and hip to toe.

There are generally six horizontal body shapes:

1. Upright triangle
2. Inverted triangle
3. Rectangle
4. Hourglass
5. Oval
6. Diamond

Now that you have processed the nine steps to style declaration you are armed with the tools to get your needs met. Pull all your declarations together into a paragraph form and read it aloud, so you can hear yourself express your needs. You now possess the language you need to ask clearly what you are looking for. All you need to do now is to put it into action. Go out there and try yourself on for size. See also "Styleguru Mantra for Solutions Inherent in You" by Pankaj Sabharwal on page 83.

## Make a Vision Board

Create the look you want by creating a vision board to capture images that resonate with you. Using a vision board affirms your focus.

What is a vision board? A vision board is a visual affirmation you create that represents all you wish to become and all you wish to have. The collage of cutout pictures, words and drawings will have a powerful purpose that will activate the law of attraction.

When you start this collage of discovery, be present, slow down and breathe. Let your creative mind flow. Go into this fun self-exploration ready to transition your inner self to your outer body. Relax, breath, focus. Have fun.

Choose a day and time that permits a peaceful environment without interruption by family, friends or the phone. This moment is about you being present and reaping the full benefit of your time. You will need:

• Poster board

• Assortment of magazines

• Glue

• Scissors

• Glitter

• Humor

Flip through your favorite style magazines and cut out the looks you love. Add words that uplift and inspire you and colors you are drawn to. Lay the cutouts on your poster board to make sure they fit and then glue them onto the poster board. I like to add glitter or scrapbooking jewels to make it pop with fun and create an authentic presentation.

Take a picture of the board and place copies by your phone, your desk and anywhere else where you can see it often.

Now that you have completed your vision board, go back to your closet and look for items that parallel the choices you have on your vision board. Ask yourself if each garment reflects who you are on your vision board.

## Retail Remorse Be Gone!

Work these rules and your wardrobe will be working for you, not you working for your wardrobe!

- Make a plan. Take inventory of items that extend your current wardrobe. This will also keep you focused on your shopping goals.

- Try shoes on mid-to-late afternoon. Your feet swell throughout the day, sometimes up to an entire size. Tight shoes make for a grumpy soul!

- The better you dress for shopping, the better your service will be.

- Match items by bringing the item with you. There are many shades of black.

- Try everything on. Returning items that do not work is a waste of time.

- If you have created a clothing allowance, bring cash only. This will help you to stay true to your budget commitment.

- Wear a good bra and a body slimmer.

- Very few items come off the rack ready to wear. Aim for a perfect fit for your body shape. Find a great tailor to help you.

- Meet the store manager. Connecting with the manager will give you direct insight to store policies. If you have a problem, it usually can be resolved quicker. Ask who their best in-store stylist is and get introduced.

If you are on a budget, buy items you can create two or three different looks from. A shift dress can be worn with a blazer for work, a pashmina for cocktails or a jean jacket for casual. Make items work for the three Cs, so you can go from corporate to cocktail to casual.

Sometimes we need to start fresh, give ourselves permission to clear away what is not working for us and simply choose again. We are all influenced by our peers, family and sales people about what does or does not look good on us. If you are clear and kind in declaring your needs and wants, you will not let yourself down. Your strength in asserting your likes and dislikes will be received with respect. You will start to enjoy shopping. Gone will be closets full of "retail regret," and, as a result, you will become a positive influence by being fearless and raising your style bar. Always remember, your best accessory is a smile.

**SHAI THOMPSON**
Image Consulting and
Chez Shai - The Style Studio

*Wear yourself well*

(250) 597-0707
shai@shaithompson.com
www.shaithompson.com

*T*IIE PURSUIT of excellence in service, to understand and surpass clients' needs is steadfast in Shai's professional presentation. She brings over 20 years of experience in fashion, marketing, sales and public relations. Her style coaching is a perfect match for her impressive business and creative background in the music industry. "Translate Your Inner Beauty to Your Outer Body" is a workshop Shai developed and is a great tool to navigate the sometimes-difficult experience of change.

In March 2011, Shai opened her home-based studio, Chez Shai, in her renovated barn in the Cowichan Valley, on Vancouver Island, Canada. Serving Vancouver Island with one-on-one style coaching and educational workshops, she enjoys the peaceful country setting.

Shai boasts a unique collection of accessories and repurposed clothes whose function is to show clients the positive difference they can make by learning about their body shape, color and style. Chez Shai is also working toward developing an earth-friendly clothing line and has worked as a senior stylist for a talent search hosted by David Foster, Nelly Furtado, Amy Foster and BJ Cook. Shai is a high energy, motivated professional, who loves serving others.

# *Suits* to Suit
## How to Make Your Suit Work for You
by Annalisa Armitage, AICI CIP

*T*HE CLASSIC suit is slowly being edged out of Western corporations since many companies favor the informality that non-suiting brings to their work force. This causes dilemmas about what is appropriate work attire as employers attempt to explain why ripped jeans, low necklines, high hemlines, T-shirts and flip-flops are unwelcome in the workplace.

The suit creates all the surety, professionalism and smartness you need for most occasions, and this chapter is all about making your suits work.

## Exactly What Is a Suit?

**For men.** A suit for a man is traditionally comprised of both a jacket and trousers in matching fabrics. There is also the three-piece suit that sports a waistcoat or vest. Each of these items can be found in a number of different styles and with different embellishments, widths and fabrics. The individual options chosen can make a suit a man's best asset or turn it into his worst enemy.

**For women.** A woman's suit can be either a trouser suit or a skirt suit. Vests or waistcoats may also be worn and the options or variety of lengths, fabrics, styles and embellishments are endless. A well-fitted suit can instantly slim the body and add credibility and stature while a poorly fitted suit can do the opposite.

> *"Like every good man, I strive for perfection, and, like every ordinary man, I have found that perfection is out of reach— but not the perfect suit."*
> —Edward Tivnan, playwright, author and journalist

## What the Right Suit Can Do for You

A suit conveys a certain formality and shows respect for yourself, your organization and your colleagues. In Western societies, a suit is the staple garment for momentous occasions, such as weddings, funerals and christenings. A suit jacket with properly padded shoulders creates a fabulous frame from which the fabric hangs. It skims over any extra weight, slims the torso and exaggerates the shoulder line. If you are short, the single line of jacket and pant together increases your apparent height. If you are slight of frame, the suit will add width at the shoulders and create an inverted, triangular silhouette. A suit can anchor your brand. A sharp suit with unique features can become your individual "uniform" for work or business.

Finally, a suit conveys authority and professionalism and is essential for ambitious corporate climbers. According to a 2010 survey of 12,000 employees in 24 countries conducted by Ipsos/Reuters Global, 37 percent of workers said that casual workers in their workplace will never make it into senior management and 66 percent responded that senior managers should always be more professionally dressed than their employees should. Given these statistics, it is important to consider carefully what you are wearing and the impression it is giving.

> *"Know, first, who you are; and then adorn yourself accordingly."*
> —Epictetus, Ancient Greek philosopher

# How a Suit Should Fit

An inexpensive suit that is a great fit is infinitely better than an ill-fitting expensive suit. A suit is an investment piece, and fit and care are critical for making your investment last. Store suits on wooden hangers that provide great support. Air and spot clean. Dry clean only when necessary—this may be as little as once every twenty to thirty wearings. Give your suit a one-day break between wearing to allow the fabric to breath. Avoid being caught in the rain since this can ruin the line of a suit and how it hangs.

## For Men

- The jacket should fit across the shoulders, and the shoulder should protrude from your shoulder no more than one centimeter or one-half inch. Any more than this amount and the suit shoulder will start to sag, giving the suit an odd-looking silhouette. The shoulder width is difficult and costly to alter, so check it first when choosing a suit.

- The placement of the waist gives the suit its dimensions, and the buttons determine the waist point. Like the shoulders of the jacket, the waist cannot be altered after the suit is made.

- The length of the jacket is up to you, and it should come down no further than the first knuckle on your fingers when your arms are at your sides. It is currently fashionable for the length to be a good deal shorter than this. However, if you have short legs in relation to your body, keep your jacket shorter to give the illusion of longer legs.

- The arms and armholes should fit snuggly without being tight. The armholes cannot be changed once the suit is made, and often less expensive suits have excessive size in the armholes to fit as many people as possible.

- Sleeve length usually can be adjusted easily, unless your suit has working sleeve buttons. It is critical to have the correct sleeve length on both sleeves. It should come down to where your hand meets your wrist. Sleeve length in relation to the shirtsleeve is most important. The shirt sleeve needs to "poke out" from beneath the jacket sleeve from one-half centimeter or one-quarter inch to two centimeters or one inch and no more, whether you are seated or standing, or have your arms bent or straight.

### For Women

- The shoulder fit is also important for women's suit jackets. Too small and it will pull and feel uncomfortable—too large and it will sag over the shoulder and look sloppy. Jacket sleeve length is not as prescribed as for men as women often wear sort sleeves underneath their jacket or a jersey top rather than a man's style shirt. If you are tall, your sleeve length should finish on the longer end of what is appropriate rather than at the shorter end, as it will look like you have outgrown the jacket. The same in reverse applies to the shorter woman—make sure the sleeve does not go past the end of your wrist.

- The length of the jacket depends on your body features. The shorter the jacket, the longer your legs will appear. If you have slim hips and legs, and you want to highlight this, choose a jacket at high-hip length. If you have large hips, choose a jacket that finishes mid-hip with a fabric that matches the jacket. If jacket and pants or skirt fabrics differ, choose a different style, longer jacket. The place where the different materials meet will create a focal point and draw the eye.

- The jacket waist needs to line up with either your natural waist or where your waist should be. Make sure the jacket button at the waist is accentuated when the jacket is buttoned. This will create the best possible silhouette.

*"Clothes can suggest, persuade, connote, insinuate, or indeed lie, and apply subtle pressure while their wearer is speaking frankly and straightforwardly of other matters."*
—Anne Hollander, American art historian and author

# What Type of Suit to Wear

**Business and casual Friday.** The most professional color combination is navy and white. It is crisp and clean and evokes subconscious thoughts of precision and control. Black can make you appear too authoritarian if you are a man, and it can strengthen a woman's image. Avoid brown suits since they must be in very fashionable styles to prevent you from appearing old-fashioned and too earthy.

If the image you wish to convey is one of credibility, capability and leadership, stick to classic styles. Avoid high fashion and trendy garments, which can make you look a little flighty and unsure of yourself, and anything that looks out of date. Again, classic styles are best. If you think classic is boring, make an outfit look more exciting by dressing up a classic suit with different accessories.

**Weddings.** Weddings give you a great opportunity to take full advantage of the benefits a suit brings and to use your creativity.

- **For men.** Unless "Black Tie" is specifically stated on the invitation, typically men can wear lighter-colored suits in a more luxurious fabric, such as wool with some silk in it. A light grey with a white or pale pink shirt and a light-colored tie evokes an elegant impression in keeping with weddings.

- **For women.** A skirt suit is typically the favored attire for the mother of the groom and mother of the bride. It achieves the formality and provides the figure advantages that only a suit can bring. Wear a camisole underneath and choose a knee-length skirt.

**Funerals.** Funerals mean different things to different people. Respect must be shown to the person who has passed and the family and friends they have left behind. Invitations rarely denote a dress code. However, a suit in a dark color, especially for men, will always be correct.

Depending on the funeral venue and the family, it may feel too business-like for a woman to wear a suit she would wear to her job, so she may wish to wear a dark dress instead. Sometimes it is the expressed wish of the departed or family that the funeral and wake be a celebration and dark colors are banned. Always respect their wishes and dress accordingly.

## Get the Look You Want in Your Suit

- **Approachable.** Lower contrasts will ensure you do not look too aggressive and authoritarian. Avoid high contrasts between your suit, shirt and tie and ensure your suit does not have bold stripes.

- **Credible.** Choose a classic, single-breasted, two-button suit in smooth, dark-colored, lightweight wool. Avoid shiny, heavily textured or light colored materials when choosing a suit. Shoes need to be darker than your suit, and socks need to match the suit. Create good contrast between your shirt and tie and your shirt and suit.

- **Assertive.** Take contrast levels up a notch. The higher the contrast, the more assertive you look. Wear a bright red tie or scarf.

- **Fun.** Add colour and a couple of patterns in accessories to make your look more fun.

- **Elegant.** Add elegance with a formal suit. Choose dark colours for the suit and pair it with a light-coloured shirt, tie, cravat or scarf. Place shiny materials, such as satin, on your lapels and or as a thin stripe down your outside leg. This will give your appearance more elegance.

> *"Women usually love what they buy, yet hate two-thirds of what is in their closets."*
> —Mignon McLaughlin, American journalist

# Quick Fixes

- **Poor quality.** A poor quality suit will often fit badly, sit badly and wear badly. You can try to have it altered. However, you cannot alter a suit too much without it looking odd, and you cannot alter the width of the shoulder or the placement of the buttons. These two things are essential to get right up front. Make sure the suit sits flat across your chest. Also, if you buy an inexpensive suit, expect it to start falling apart earlier than a more expensive suit. Repair or replace a suit at the first sign of wear.

- **Poor fit.** An ill-fitting suit is worse than a poor-quality suit. Choose a suit that fits your shoulders and has the correct length. Make sure the placement of the waist button is on your waist or just below it. The length of a jacket can only be changed slightly, and the shoulders and button placement cannot be changed at all. Trousers can only be taken in a maximum of two inches or five centimeters.

- **Wrong style for body shape.** There are dozens of different body shapes for men and women. However, it is not only general body shapes to take into consideration. You may have different body parts you want hidden or minimized.

It is said that the ideal body shape for women is an hourglass, where your upper body is in proportion to your lower body, and there is some definition in the waist. An upper half that is bigger than the lower half is also a desirable shape. Model Elle McPherson has made this shape almost as preferable as the hourglass. If your lower half is bigger than your upper half, try bulking up your upper half while slimming or hiding your hips. Wearing a structured suit jacket helps with this.

For men, the best shape is the inverted triangle where your upper body is bigger than your lower body. Suits are good for creating this shape, with the structured shoulder giving the impression of wider shoulders.

- **Poor handling.** Try not to dry clean your suits often since the process deteriorates the suit quickly. Always wear something under your suit, so it never touches your body in places where you perspire. If your suit is soiled from the outside, try to spot clean the soiled area before getting it dry-cleaned. Ironing a suit with an iron that is too hot can make the suit shiny in spots, ruining the look of the suit. Avoid ironing by hanging your suit correctly and giving it at least one day of rest between wearing it. If you need to iron a suit, make sure the iron is not too hot. Cover the suit with a fine cotton cloth, and never directly touch a woolen suit with an iron.

- **Wrong fabric choice.** Most suit fabrics are rated with a weight in grams or ounces. If a suit is less than 250 grams or 7 ounces, it is a "summer weight" and only good for hot climates. Fabric between 250 grams and 350 grams, or 7 to 10 ounces, is lightweight and can be used all year in most climates. Fabric above 450 grams or 10 ounces would be considered a heavyweight fabric and is only good for winter in reasonably cold climates. Fabric colours and patterns can also be seasonal. Some light grays and beiges can only be worn in summer while some tweeds can only be worn in winter. There are, however, good ranges of fabrics that can be worn all year.

Everyone needs at least one classic suit. In the right color, style, fit and fabric to suit your body shape, coloring and purpose, it will long outlast any other item you own. The pieces also have the added advantage of being able to be worn together or singly, depending on the weather or the purpose. See also "Are You Ready for Your Close-up?" by Thea Wood on page 25.

If you can afford it, get your suit custom-made by someone who can guarantee the fit and guarantee that you will be happy with it. Even though some off-the-rack brand name suits are more expensive, you will get a better suit if it is tailor-made for you. Some tailors will not only guarantee the suit fits well, they will also ensure the style is right for your body shape and the color is right for your coloring.

If you decide to buy a suit from a retail store, do a bit of research and look at what the shop assistants are wearing. Do they look like they would fit in your business with their clothing? Ask other people for advice, especially people whom you consider well dressed.

This perfect suit may seem like a large investment—however, when you divide the total cost by the number of times you will wear it, and again by the number of compliments you will get, you will quickly realize a return on your investment. The only challenge is how many more suits you should have and when to stop buying them.

**ANNALISA ARMITAGE,** AICI CIP

+61 413898776
annalisa@myimageconsultant.com.au
www.myimageconsultant.com.au
www.myownpersonalbrand.com

*A*NNALISA ARMITAGE lives in Sydney, Australia, and has done what many dream to do by following her passion. She left the corporate world in 2006 where she was extremely successful, but unfulfilled, to become a highly respected entrepreneur. She is driven by the motto, "Life is too short and contains too many exciting possibilities to let how you look stand in your way."

She has appeared on national television, is sought after for her opinions on professional attire and other image-related matters, and contributes to a weekly column for the Daily Telegraph called "What to Where?" She set up My Own Personal Brand to create clothing without compromise and individually tailored, beautifully fitting, unique clothing for her clients to set them apart and demonstrate their individuality.

Annalisa is a professional speaker and has worked in training, coaching and running workshops since the 1990's. Most of all, Annalisa is a down-to-earth, fun-loving, warm-hearted person who puts people at ease very quickly. Her clients, first and foremost, have fun when they work with her.

# Accessorize! Accessorize!
## *Accessorize!*

by Veronica T. H. Purvis, MS, AICI FLC

ACCESSORIES ARE as important as your clothes and can actually be more essential in establishing your image and brand. Just as clothes can convey your lifestyle, personality and preferences, accessories take you to the next level and further demonstrate your sense of style and your attention to detail. They complete your wardrobe and give you the opportunity to express yourself in creative ways. Accessories can set you apart and display your individuality. Regardless if you are a man or woman, you can use accessories to your advantage in almost any circumstance, whether it is for your profession or your personal life. What are accessories? When I talk about accessories, I am not just talking about earrings and necklaces. While these are integral pieces, accessories are almost anything other than your clothing top and bottom. Accessories include:

- Belts and suspenders
- Bracelets and watches
- Brooches and pins
- Cufflinks
- Earrings and necklaces
- Eyewear
- Handbags and briefcases
- Handkerchiefs
- Hats
- Headbands, barrettes, clips
- Leg coverings such as stockings, tights, socks, knee highs
- Nose rings, eyebrow rings and jewel appliqués
- Rings
- Shoes
- Ties, scarfs and shawls
- Umbrellas

There are several accessories that men and women should have and carefully select. One accessory that everyone needs in his or her wardrobe is a belt. One or two versatile belts that work with most jeans, slacks and skirts are a good start. Remember that if your belt loops are visible in your outfit, then a belt must be worn. Every man needs to own a few nice ties that can be worn to the office, an evening out or to a formal event. Every woman needs to invest in a well-made handbag since it is one of the main accessories that accompanies you everywhere.

> *"Accessories are important and becoming more and more important every day."*
> —Giorgio Armani, Italian fashion designer

## Accessories Are Part of Your Brand

Accessories can help establish your brand if you use them in a strategic manner. Branding, or personal branding as discussed here, is the purposeful positioning of yourself to exemplify a clear and consistent image and message that demonstrates your individuality and your value. To use accessories to your branding advantage:

• Begin with an honest assessment of who you are and what you stand for. For example, an attorney who represents refugees would choose different accessories than an attorney who represents multinational corporations.

• Ask yourself—and others if it helps—what perceptions you convey and what you want to convey. If you want to convey classic or a traditional image, then a nose ring may not be the way to go. However, pearl jewelry may do the trick.

• Decide if your current image, including your appearance, behavior and communication, matches your personal branding goals. They all have to work in unison else you risk sending conflicting messages. If you are unsure of your current total image, I can provide an assessment, a complete overhaul or image update if necessary.

- Determine what is missing or out of sync and address it. Maybe it is just your verbal and non-verbal communication that does not match your appearance. It is never too late to enhance your communication skills. See also "Savvy Interaction" by Katrina Van Dopp on page 37.

- Decide what will distinguish you from your peers socially and professionally. Sometimes, it takes an outsider or an objective perspective to help determine this. Do not be afraid to seek the advice of other trusted sources.

Remember that everything you do and own plays a role in your personal branding. Your clothes, your car, your job, your friends, your social events, your house, décor and more are all part of your brand. Each of these things reflects your personality and, therefore, your brand. Begin to consider ways to creatively extend your brand through accessories.

You may find that you naturally gravitate to a particular accessory. Maybe you love wearing watches or you love pendants. Look at the accessories you like wearing and examine why you like them, what they say about you and how you may be able to utilize them to your benefit.

Famous examples of personal branding via accessories include former United States Secretary of State Madeline Albright for her brooches. Former mayor of Washington, D.C., Anthony Williams was one of the few political figures who consistently wore various bow ties with his button-down cotton shirts. On a high level, bow ties can convey excellence and intelligence. The former mayor wearing a bow tie instantly communicated his brand image of excellence and intelligence.

Many entertainers have strategically used their attire and accessories to instantly convey their image, including Lady Gaga with her extreme costumes, wigs and shoes, Elton John and his eyeglasses, Liberace and his outfits, Rihanna and her hair and Michael Jackson and his glove.

This list goes on and on with entertainers who have found ways to help symbolize their image with one or more key accessories.

Maybe one of the more contemporary visible icons is United States First Lady Michelle Obama. She is known for having a stylish wardrobe, and one of the reasons she is recognized as a modern style icon is her use of accessories. Her wardrobe is not usually flashy. However, she uses accessories to make a recycled piece in her wardrobe look different, to add drama and glamour to her ensemble or to add more interest to a basic look. Her flexibility and creativity with accessorizing has helped her image appear modern, fresh, stylish and smart. See also "Who Are You?" by Sharon J. Geraghty on page 1 for more information on branding.

## Use Accessories to Distinguish Yourself

After you have determined what your personal brand is, you need to determine how you can convey that brand through your image and how it can be reinforced via accessories. Here are ways you can use accessories in your professional and personal life to distinguish yourself.

For example, if you are in the social advocate field, such as a social worker, consider how accessories might help set you apart. Let us assume you have done a color and clothes assessment to determine that adding more varieties of color to your wardrobe makes you seem more accessible and open to clients and colleagues. You have added warm- and soft-colored tops to your wardrobe. Next, you want to set yourself apart from your colleagues and others in your industry, and you can do that with accessories.

Consider adding a flower pin or brooch to your wardrobe. You could wear a flower of various types and colors in your hair, pin it to your jacket lapel or add it to a silk cord and wear it around your neck like a choker. This could become your signature look. You might add an open

-hands symbol to your ensembles in the form of pendants, necklaces and so on to strengthen your brand as a social worker.

These types of touches add interest to your wardrobe and can become a signature look if you consistently incorporate them. When done consistently, these accessories become your personal logo, so choose them carefully.

*"It is the...unforgettable, ultimate accessory of fashion that heralds your arrival and prolongs your departure."*
—Coco Chanel, French fashion designer

# Accessories and Your Body

You can use accessories to accentuate your body type. Different types of accessories can be strategically used to make you appear slimmer, longer, fuller or shorter, whatever your goal. Below is a list with different body types and what accessories should be used to balance your figure. Usually, the goal is to make your body seem proportioned— accessories do this if used properly. Below are examples and tips to accomplish this.

## Accessorizing Tips

### Petite/Slim Frame

• Wear smaller jewelry that does not overpower your frame.

• Wear thinner belts that will not overwhelm your frame.

• Carry smaller purses that do not overshadow your body.

•Wear smaller shoes/heels, like kitten heals or petite platforms (yes— there is such a thing), that will not make your legs look skinnier than they already are.

• Wear shorter (medium to short) hairstyles that show off your face and frame instead of distracting from them.

**Tall/Plus-Size Frame**

• Wear slightly larger jewelry pieces, such as substantial necklaces, chunky bracelets.

• Wear wider belts to give the illusion of a slimmer waist and body.

• Wear more substantial shoes and heels, not in height, but in sole size/width—so no kitten heels.

• Wear longer hair to minimize your body frame.

Remember that hair is an accessory. Hair is one of the first things that is noticed about a person. The style, color and length all speak volumes about a person's health, attention to detail, fashion sense and more.

Take the time and money to invest in a hairstyle that compliments your face shape, lifestyle and personality. In general, a shorter hairstyle (that exposes most of the neck) becomes slimmer and petite frames because it highlights and brings more emphasis to the body's curves, whereas longer hair (past the neck) can provide more balance for a heavier frame. In other words, longer hair can overpower a small frame because a lot of hair can make your body appear smaller.

A general rule for other accessories is to keep in mind that bare skin is going to make the area appear longer and/or bigger. For example, if you have bare arms with no jewelry, your arms are going to appear longer than if you wear bracelets and jewelry on your wrist. The same goes for your neck area—the space will appear greater and possibly longer when you wear no necklace than when you do (and vice versa—you can also wear certain necklaces that elongate your neck). Also, if you have a small frame, keep accessories in proportion and choose smaller pieces, such as a thinner belt, petite jewelry, and smaller handbags and shoes. You do not want to overwhelm your frame and appear smaller than you already are. The opposite is true if you have a larger frame. In that case, your frame can support bigger, more substantial accessories, such as a larger bag, bigger jewelry pieces and more substantial shoes and heels. These things will make you appear a little smaller compared to your accessories.

Nails are noticed too and need to be kept neat, clean and well shaped. For professional settings, avoid too long or too short nails, as both look unprofessional. For social settings, you can do creative things with nails with all the innovations in nail care, such as the magnetic illusions, different shapes and various patterns and prints.

Fragrances such as perfumes and colognes can also be considered accessories. Match your fragrance to your image. If your overall brand screams sophistication, then avoid wearing a fragrance made for teens. Keep in mind that the fragrance you wear on weekends may not be appropriate for work if it is overly sultry.

## Accessory Don'ts

Some people tend to over accessorize, which is just as bad as not knowing how to accessorize at all. There are different tips to help you not overdo it. Fashion designer Coco Chanel suggested you take off the last item you put on. There are point systems available to help you stay below a certain number of accessories. One easy rule of thumb I would offer is to have one central piece that is center stage. So if you are wearing show-stopping earrings, do not wear a dramatic necklace that competes with the earrings. Your accessories should not be fighting for attention, but rather they should all blend and complement one another. You never want to look like you stepped out of the house with all of your favorite accessories on at once, such as a chunky necklace, dangling earrings, a long scarf plus a giant leopard bag!

## Communicate with Accessories

Regardless of your profession, lifestyle and personality, accessories can be incorporated into your wardrobe without seeming forced or inauthentic. The key is to find the accessories that match your personal image and then have fun with them when the occasion calls for it, such as at parties and social gatherings.

You can accessorize for both professional and personal events. Accessories may have to be scaled back for work and emphasized more in social settings. Be creative and consider non-conventional items to use as accessories. In addition to the ones already mentioned, think about gloves and walking canes.

Try new things with your accessories, like wearing your jewelry in a different way than you normally do. Do not be afraid to try something new. Use scarves in various ways and places. Instead of wearing it around your neck, use it as a belt and lace it through your belt loops or just tie it around your waist with a dress.

The best strategies in personally branding yourself with accessories is to first determine who you are and what you want to be by conducting an internal and external personal brand assessment. Second, find out what accessory or accessories fit your personality, profession and lifestyle. Next, choose items that set you apart and help serve as your signature look and personal logo. Lastly, make sure the accessory is unique to you and not easily copied or mimicked.

**VERONICA T. H. PURVIS,** MS, AICI FLC
**Vera Iconica,** LLC

*Realize your true image*

(301) 404-6968
vp@veraiconica.com
www.veraiconica.com

*V*ERONICA T.H. PURVIS, MS, AICI FLC, is a certified image consultant and founder of Vera Iconica, LLC, an innovative and forward-thinking provider of image improvement products and services in the Washington, D.C., area. Vera Iconica, LLC, which means true image, helps others find their true image and upgrade their style and communication in their professional and personal lives. Veronica provides personal and professional image coaching to adults, youth and businesses.

As an author, writer and speaker, Veronica is committed to transforming others' lives. Personal consultations include wardrobe consultations, training in hair and nails, accessories consulting, interviewing preparation and more. Comprehensive appearance, communication and business etiquette (ACE) training is also available. Veronica helps people realize their true image so they can attain their full potential.

Veronica holds a bachelor of arts in communication and a master of science in management and marketing. She is a graduate of the John Casablanca's Modeling and Career Center and has worked in media production behind and in front of the camera and has acted in films. She also served as VP communication on the AICI Washington, D.C., chapter board of directors.

# *Love* the Space You're In
## Creating the Space that Reflects Who You Are

by Linnore Gonzales, CID, Green AP

*Y*OUR SPACE is who you are. It is a reflection of your creativity, passion and spirit. In today's busy world, it is important to have a space to go to unwind, relax and feel good. Imagine a space that has all your favorite things that you love that make you comfortable, happy and "at home." Does your space make you feel airy, calm and alive? Does your space say YOU? If not, this chapter will help you create a space that does. If so, this chapter will help you enhance your environment to become even more "you."

Figuring out your design personality and style can be intimidating. Creating that space to reflect your personality and style is even more daunting. Deciding on how to decorate the space, how to start and where to start is not an easy task. With a literally unending variety of choices available in choosing a style, color scheme and overall look, creating the space you love can be overwhelming. So, how do you get started?

First, find out what your design style is. Then map out a plan to create a decorating plan for your style and create that space you will love.

On the next page, are some popular styles:

- **Asian Style** decor uses a clean and linear, elegant and uncluttered look. Natural elements are used in the decor to create a calm oasis and tranquil spa-like feel.

- **Beach Style** decor is described as comfortable and airy and is one of the most budget-friendly styles.

- **Cottage Style or Shabby Chic** gravitates toward vintage and sentimental elements to create a comfortable and family-friendly space.

- **Contemporary Style** uses bold furnishings and clean lines. This style may be for you if you are drawn to dramatic finishes and like rooms that have an artistic flair.

- **Country Style** is not just American flags, shaker chairs and hearts. Because it came about in the high courts of European royalty, country-style furnishings and decor are often quite refined.

- **Eclectic Style** is good if you love to mix and match things and have a flair for pulling it off.

- **French Country Style** is for you if you like casual elegance, sunny splashes of color and natural and rustic accessories that can remind you of your summers in France.

- **Modern Style** is often a misunderstood style, yet a beautiful one because its' roots are strongly grounded in art and architecture. If you like simple, uncluttered spaces with clean lines and a lack of fussy adornments, then this style is for you.

- **Southwestern Style** is for you if you want warm and down-to-earth spaces. The color turquoise, terra cotta tiles and timbered ceilings are some main elements of this style.

- **Traditional Style** is for you if you prefer calm and comfortable and if you avoid flashy or cluttered decor. Traditional style is the most popular decorating and design style.

- **Transitional Style** decorating is a balanced combination of traditional and contemporary, so if stylish sophistication is what you are looking for, this style may just be for you.

- **Tropical Island Style** is another one of the misunderstood styles. A room decorated tropical island style is not necessarily filled with fake palm trees and Hawaiian print. This elegant style celebrates the customs of the Pacific Island people.

- **Tuscan Style** is for those of you who dream about sun-drenched days in Southern Italy.

- **Victorian Style** is ornate, rich, opulent and expensive.

## Discover Your Decorating Style

As you can see from the above, there are tons of decorating styles, so it can be a bit confusing and intimidating to understand all of them. However, knowing what styles you prefer and are drawn to will help you have a cohesive look and feel in your space. Even if you are clueless when it comes to recognizing different decorating styles, you can still easily identify certain items in your space that you enjoy. Go around your space and make a note of your favorite things that inspire and make you happy. Take photos of these things as you take inventory. Do you have sentimental items? What do you like about your favorite things? Do the lines of the items or perhaps the color grab your attention? Do you like the pattern or texture of the item? Are you attracted to it because of how it reflects light? For example, one of our clients has a sentimental Japanese kimono that we framed and used as the focal point in one of her rooms. We picked out and used the colors in the kimono throughout her space.

As you take a fresh look at your space, do you notice if you avoid bright colors or do you love them? Is your space decorated with a lot of photos and accessories or do you prefer a more streamlined and less decorated space? What about your furniture? Do you have clean lines or are you more attracted to fluff and comfort?

**Define your lifestyle.** If you are single, your space will look a lot different than the space of a family with four kids and a dog. Though you may love and appreciate the spaces you see in decorating and lifestyle magazines, you should be honest with yourself about what works for you and your lifestyle. When defining your lifestyle, ask yourself these questions: What are you planning to do in this space? How much upkeep will you be willing or have time to do? How many people will need to live in the space and how are they going to utilize the space? What is the flow of traffic through your space? What available lighting do you have that will work for your needs?

**Define the existing style.** If you live in a Victorian style house, it might look a bit off if it has Asian or a very contemporary interior decor. If you purchased this style house, chances are you chose it because you were attracted to it, liked it and felt good about it. To carry the Victorian style inside your home, you can introduce ornate, rich and "expensive" looking pieces. Using clean lines and modern furnishings inside that will be typical of an Asian or contemporary style might not be a good flow from the outside look of your home to the inside decoration. It is not a rule to follow the style of the home when you decorate the inside. However, too much contrast and difference between the outside and the inside will look out of place and may even be uncomfortable.

**Define your region.** Where do you live? Always consider the style and climate where you reside. If you live in Colorado, you do not have to go all out Western or decorate with a mountain lodge look, but it will help to pay attention to availability of certain decor in your area. Also, consider the ground around your home during various seasons because that is what is going to be tracked inside your home. For example, a white entryway carpet may not make sense and may not be practical in a snowy upstate New York suburb home.

Once you know what your decorating style is, you are now ready to create your decorating plan. A plan is essential to keep you on track with your style and what works for your space. A plan is your road map and will keep you from unnecessary purchases and huge decorating mistakes, and it keeps you on track with your timeline and budget.

## Creating a Decorating Plan for Your Style

Once you have defined your style, clarified your existing needs and evaluated your surroundings and functionality of the space, you are now ready to make your list.

**Start with your wish list.** When creating this list, remember to make it a reasonable and attainable wish list and not one that has things you wish for but cannot reasonably afford to have. List things you can feasibly do and purchase if you had more than what you would normally spend on that item. For instance, write down things that your current closet does not provide you and how you would build your next closet differently. Do not write, "gut master closet and start from scratch." Be specific. If you would like your closet to have more shelf space, write that down.

If your wish list ends up to be so extensive that it would cost you a lot of money to get your space the way you want it, then your current space may not be one that suits you. At this point you may be better off putting your hard earned cash into another space that is more your style.

**Review and narrow your wish list.** Take a close, hard look at your wish list. Note the top five things that you really want to see happen. Mark the ones that are impractical and do not fit into your lifestyle. Consider what can be achieved in a reasonable amount of time for a reasonable price. As you narrow down your list, do not neglect to leave on something that may be impractical but can give you great pleasure. You never know what you can make happen as you work through your project.

**Create your budget.** Look at the top five things and consider your budget. What things can you do on your own and what items need to be outsourced? Write prices beside each of the items. Be realistic. Do not assign $500 for new state-of-the-art appliances when you know this is not realistic. Are there one or two items on your top five that you can possibly do right now? Break them down and make sure to assign individual budgets. When you realize that you cannot complete your top five, then break it down into mini phases.

**Make your goal list.** After you have taken a good long look at your desires and your budget, it is now time to write down the first room or project you'd like to complete as your first item on your goal list. Work your way through your top, doable and affordable wish list items and write them down in the order of how you would like to complete them. Remember that you are in control of your goal list and not the other way around. You are able to modify your goal list as you go through the project. As you complete some projects or rooms, some of your goals may resolve themselves and become less of a priority.

**Start putting it all together.** You now know your style and have created your list. The next step is to put it all together to finalize your decorating plan. As with any business plan, you should start with a written statement for your project. Whether you decide to tackle a large project or start with one room in your home, it always helps to have a plan on paper. Remember to clearly identify the style, timeline and budget. Start with what you have and find that inspiration piece or color scheme.

Not everyone can start with a fresh, empty room. Most people already have pieces of furniture in their homes, architectural features that they may have to live with or things that they may not be able to change. Focus on what you like and make them important. Find ways to downplay and camouflage things that you do not want and cannot change.

Purchase a single accordion folder or binder to help keep you organized and on track as you work through your decorating project. File everything in here from your goal list for the project, the budget, color scheme, paint samples, floor plans to furniture layout, fabric swatches, stone, wood and carpet samples to photos and any lighting plan. Everything that has to do with your project is filed in the folder or binder.

**Now the fun begins.** Do you start with the flooring first or do you pick a color scheme before you add any furniture and accessories? Things can get tricky when you have items already in your space. In an empty room, it is a great decorating practice to start with the backdrop before purchasing furniture. In this instance, decide on the flooring or paint color first before adding the furniture and accessory items. If you do not have a clean slate to start with, you should find your inspiration piece.

Where do you find your inspiration? Did we already mention that decorating is not an easy task? With all the options available in the marketplace, you can easily be distracted and intimidated. Look around you and try to get inspired. You will be surprised at the number of places where interior decorating inspiration can be found.

- **Decorating magazines.** Look at a bunch of different ones and check out what designers and other homeowners are doing. Do not limit yourself to magazines that you normally gravitate to. Looking at other magazines that focus on different styles is a great way to be exposed to styles you may not think of and be surprised you may like.

- **Travel.** Get inspired when you travel. Pay attention to different things you see when you travel to different places. Bring home a piece you love that you can use as your inspiration piece.

- **Fashion and textile.** Fashions and fabrics are great sources of inspiration. Do you like the pattern on an old sweater or the texture on a throw? Do you have a favorite dress? Think about the look and feel of the item and design your room around it. Consider color, pattern, textures and style.

- **Nature.** The colors found in flowers, leaves, stones, trees and everything else in nature could be a source of inspiration. Your inspiration does not have to be complicated—sometimes the best ideas come from the simplest things. The pink you see on a flower might be the perfect shade for your bedroom walls. The particular green found in a single leaf can be the perfect jumping off point for your family room.

- **Movies and television.** Next time you watch television, pay attention to the set design. The homes, hotels and offices featured in movies and TV shows are stunning and can be a source of your inspiration.

- **Packaging.** Have you noticed the packaging that comes with the products you buy? A lot of thought goes into packaging products to appeal to people. You may get inspired by the color, look and feel of a particular packaging. For example, the Hermes® famous orange packaging can inspire you to use the color as an accent or the robin's egg blue you find on Tiffany® boxes can be the perfect chair color.

Inspiration can be found all around us. Take your camera with you everywhere you go. With phones now equipped with cameras, it is so easy to snap a picture any time you see something you like and are attracted to. Even if you do not know how you will use it, it might come in handy when you are searching for decorating ideas.

Whether you chose to hire a designer to assist you in decorating your space or go about doing it on your own, following the steps above is crucial to creating the space that you will love.

Your home is you and is yours. The decision on how to proceed and what needs to be done is what you want, need and desire. Trust your instincts. Take your time. Do not be pressured to make hasty decisions that can cause costly mistakes. Go with what you love, and in the end you will create a space that you absolutely love!

**LINNORE GONZALES,** CID, Green AP

*Love the space you're in!*

(303) 346-2593
lgonzales@decorandyou.com
www.decorandyouhr.com

*O*WNER OF Decor & You®, Linnore Gonzales believes that everyone should love the space they are in. In addition to Decor & You, Linnore is a licensee of Exciting Windows!™, the nation's authoritative one-stop resource for window fashion experts. She also owns a long-term part-time staffing company in the metro Denver region called 10 til 2, a community magazine and a TV production company.

Creating the space you love can be very intimidating and overwhelming. By listening to clients and building that special relationship with them, Linnore is able to create a personalized Decor Plan™ that is tailored to the client's individual tastes, needs, budget and timeframe to help them achieve the results desired and avoid costly decorating mistakes.

An active member of various chamber and women's organizations, Linnore contributes decorating articles to local publications. She is also the host of her own Internet radio program and of a weekly local decorating television show, *Good Living by Design.* A certified Green Accredited Professional by the Sustainable Furnishings Council, Linnore and her team sustainably designed and furnished an energy freedom home that was featured in the 2011 Parade of Homes in Colorado.

# Be Technologically *Savvy*

by Karen Kennedy

ODAY, WITH so much electronic communication, such as email, texting, Facebook®, Twitter®, LinkedIn® and other social media platforms for connecting with people, it's no wonder many of us do not know exactly what is appropriate to best represent ourselves online. Have you ever seen a section on online etiquette in a user manual? I do not think so. Not to worry! This chapter will share with you the dos and don'ts of communicating using different online media. Soon, you will know if pushing "send" is a good idea after you have uploaded that photo, made that comment or posted to that blog.

In my company, Lady Blossoms, I focus on three areas with my clients: self, style and space. All three of these apply to what you do online. Your Facebook or LinkedIn page is your electronic space. With every keystroke you post, you are presenting yourself and your style online. Presenting self through technology includes correspondence via email, text messaging, instant messaging, posting to social networks and other online social media platforms.

Remember in school when you learned how to write cursive, then to type and format a letter and review your work for grammatical errors? Now there is a completely new set of skills to learn. You need to know how to email, text, interact on social networking sites and even tweet effectively. Today, these skills are just as important as everything you learned in freshman English!

Like it or not, people will judge you by the quality of your speech, whether verbal or written. In the case of technology, knowing how to speak the language of these new forms of communication is absolutely the smart and savvy way to be the social sensation you are. It is a bit like ordering coffee. You would not speak "Starbucks®" at Peet's Coffee® by ordering a vente caramel macchiato because you know only Starbucks uses the term "venti."

We will learn and discuss all the different methods of communication and a few of the most popular ways to KIT (keep in touch) with our family, friends and business associates. Let's get started.

## Text It

Text messaging is becoming the most popular way of communicating. In a 2011 webinar hosted by Neustar®, it was reported that 2.5 billion text messages are sent every day and more text messages are sent per phone than phone calls.

Text messaging is instant communication between two people using cell phones. It is the equivalent of IM (instant messaging) on your computer. Here is a great rule of thumb for text messaging: KISS it—Keep It Simple and Straightforward when you text. There is nothing worse than hearing the new text message chime on your phone and looking down to read a long, convoluted text message. As a friend of mine said, "I don't want to read a whole book!"

Think of texting as a fast way to communicate a little bit of information. Did you know that most smart phones come with pre-stored text messages, such as "On my way," or "I'm running late," "In a meeting," or "I will call you later"?

Of course, we are not speaking in absolutes here, and this does not apply to everyone reading this or each person you text. It is your responsibility to know your audience. That is, ask a new acquaintance the best way to get in contact with him or her. For example, I have a client who absolutely hates texting. He despises the little screen and having to scroll through the letters. On the other hand, I know texting is a great way for me to drop a quick line to my man to pick up more eggs on his way home from work. Knowing your audience is key here because many people still cannot "speak" text slang. Your "brb," or "otl til 2" (be right back, out to lunch until 2 o'clock) will have them looking at their phone as though they were trying to figure out the *Chronicle's*® Sunday paper crossword puzzle!

**1.** Be extra nice—the person reading the message cannot hear the tone of your voice. Using "smiley" faces helps to communicate your tonality.

**2.** Send your messages with a KISS: Keep It Simple and Straightforward.

**3.** Do not send too many text messages. By the fifth message, pick up the phone.

**4.** Ask people which form of communication they prefer. Not everyone is the same, and no single form of communication should be taken for granted.

**5.** Learn common text verbiage. Once you begin to text, you have a responsibility to understand the language you are using.

**6.** Edit your text messages before you send them! Sometimes, the auto-correct feature incorrectly chooses a word for you. Do a quick review of your message before you send it.

**7.** Avoid typing in ALL CAPS. In the dialect of texting, all caps implies yelling or excitement. If your intention is neither, turn the caps off.

**8.** Avoid exclamation points unless you are yelling or excited. Heavy use of exclamations can be a huge annoyance.

**9.** Be mindful of the person you are texting. If you are texting during school or work hours, limit your texting to a time when they aren't running a risk of being inappropriate wherever they are.

**10.** Know your audience and do not use too many abbreviations when texting.

# Email It

Email literally means "electronic mail" and should be structured the way a letter delivered through the USPS (United States Postal Service) would be. It should have a greeting, body of information and a closing, at the very least. Just as if you are emailing your BFF (best friend forever), greet your friends when you initiate contact with them.

- Be sure to begin your email with a greeting, such as "Dear" for formal emails and "Hi" for informal ones.

- Use spell check. It is difficult and annoying to read a paragraph full of run-on sentences and grammatical errors.

- Structure your email with paragraph spacing to make for an easy and more appealing read.

- A short description in the subject line gives people an idea of what the email is about. Jogging the memory of a new acquaintance with a topic in the subject line will ensure they open it rather than overlook it as spam.

- Choose an email address that is simple for others to remember and appropriate enough to send to First Lady Michelle Obama. It is best for your email address to be simple and easily identify you. It is not a good idea to apply for a job with the email address "reppingthebay415." An employer or even a person of interest may frown on the way you chose to present yourself. Some people have separate work and personal accounts. This is a great option if you do not want to commingle your professional and personal contacts.

- Elevate the presentation of yourself in all ways with a KISS (Keep It Simple and Straightforward).

- Read your emails and correct any grammatical and/or punctuation errors as needed.

- Do not forward chain emails to others unless you can personally vouch for the information in an email (for example, you know and trust the family of someone fundraising for medical bills).

- Clean up email before sending. In the case of forwarding, delete all email addresses and any unnecessary content.

- If you are sending an attachment, be sure it is attached! This simple error may come across as amateur.

- Remember your audience and decide accordingly if emoticons :<) or abbreviations are appropriate to use.

## Connecting Through Social Networks

Social media such as Facebook, Twitter and LinkedIn keep us connected to many "friends" around the world. This is your chance to be the life of the party without putting on 4-inch heels and regretting it in the morning! Herein lies the question: What is appropriate online?

Some people think anything goes and that they are expressing themselves freely. However, if you would not do or say something in person, then it is best not to do or say it online either! For those of you who would say or do it in person, just remember that everyone sees what you put on your social media sites. Therefore, if you befriended Grandma last month, she will probably be shocked and appalled to see her darling granddaughter posed provocatively in her Facebook profile picture or any other picture online.

Facebook has made it super easy to set up your account. You choose who can see or what they can say on your page. Take the time to change the settings and maintain the level of respect and integrity you want from your family, friends, coworkers and business connections, respectively. On the same note, you also must hold yourself to a standard of dignity and respect online and in person. When someone sees you in person, you would not want them to be thinking about the online picture of you partying in Mexico on the beach.

Be discreet with your private business. There was a story in the news of a home of a young woman that had been burglarized while she was out of town. The thieves took everything and seemed to have known the best time to do it. Why do you think that was? That's right! She posted online when, where and how long she was going to be out of town. The thieves must have been thinking, "This is too easy. This is a piece of cake!" Moral of the story? Do not post the details of your life online, especially *before* an event takes place.

Again, KISS your friends and family with your presence and leave something to the imagination. You surely do not want to come off as boastful and self-centered. Incorporate words of inspiration, stimulating conversation, intriguing news articles and post events that will help others to better themselves. Try something like, "The next Women's Business Conference is coming up in April. Anyone interested in going? Inbox me!"

- Do not post pictures of you that can be frowned upon or be mis-construed. Keep it PG-rated and you won't be embarrassed or find yourself having to explain it to your employer or family.

- Do not post messages that show you are bored and have nothing better to do.

- Take advantage of setting up accounts so your business friends are separate from your friends. This will ensure content for the designated group goes only to them.

- Do not engage in arguments with people on social sites. If there is a matter that needs to be addressed, be mature, take the conversation offline and contact that person personally, without subjecting all of your family and friends to the matter. No schoolyard fights online.

- Do not post every detail of your life online, especially information that could jeopardize your safety or that of others.

- Edit your posts before you hit the send button.

- Ask permission before posting and tagging people in places and pictures online.

- Do not be judgmental and allow people to have their own opinions.

- Post newsworthy information that is beneficial to your audience.

## Be Tech Smart and Socially Savvy!

Whether in person or online, you want to present yourself in your best light and give others a reason to want to stay in touch with you. Create communication that will be valued by others because you took the time to understand how to effectively communicate—and in a way that supports your message being fully received. Talk to people the same way you would if they were in the same room with you. Greet them, deliver your message concisely with courtesy and use a closing. Following these simple guidelines will help you get the results you want in your virtual communication with others!

**KAREN KENNEDY**
Social Etiquette Coach and Speaker
Lady Blossoms

*Appropriately Present Your Self,
Style and Space*

(415) 735-LADY (5239)
www.ladyblossoms.net
info@ladyblossoms.net

KAREN KENNEDY founded Lady Blossoms Social Etiquette Program and Services in spring 2011. What started out as a social etiquette program for women has evolved to full-service offerings to enhance self, style and space for both men and women. Her clients have a resource for fine tuning themselves professionally and personally, as well as creating a style and personal space that speaks what they want others to hear and see.

Working with Karen is always a pleasure. Helping others achieve their personal best exudes in the quality and care she puts into each client and project. After working with Karen, your natural self, style or space will speak the way you have always wanted. Her clients are more confident about themselves, excited to go home or entertain in their newly decorated homes, and are more outgoing with their new unique style.

Karen has mentored young women for more than fifteen years. She has been instrumental in the community, volunteering time and service. Her work history and personal experiences have ranged from nonprofit women's shelters to Fortune 500® investment powerhouses. Karen's course of study has included social and behavioral science and communications.

# The *Etiquette* of Dining

by Anita Shower

*T*HERE IS such grace, pomp and circumstance associated with the fine art of dining. Dining brings our senses to a full throttle when we know we are about to enjoy a special dinner, either in our home, in a restaurant or with friends in their home. It begins with choosing the appropriate clothes for the evening, then moves on to employing our imagination about the decorations and then to our delighting in the endless possibilities of the courses encompassing the menu. What an evening to look forward to!

Dining etiquette prepares you for many situations in business and in life. When you understand the "rules," you will appear more confident and will be more confident since you will know what to do! Whether we are talking about a table setting or how to pass the salt and pepper, the rules and rituals of dining etiquette add grace and elegance to our all-too-often-ordinary lives. They are part of being socially smart and savvy!

Dining with sterling silver flatware, fine china on a charger plate, candlelight and appropriate music are the details often remembered during an evening that is perfectly orchestrated. The table, when appropriately set, includes the flatware, the china and the appropriate stemware—all where they belong! There is service on the right for coffee or tea, as well. A linen napkin completes the ensemble. See also "Love the Space You're In!" by Linnore Gonzales on page 135.

## The Fine Dining Table

With fine dining, the table is set with a tablecloth. The sterling silver flatware and china are placed in a particular order and are part of the table setting. Silverware is to be used in order, from the outside in. As I always say, "Pieces of flatware are not weapons of mass destruction!"

- The salad fork is on the left, from the outside in toward the plate. The spent salad fork is left on the salad plate, so both fork and plate are removed together.

- The entree fork is next to the salad fork.

- To the right of the charger plate, you will find the knife with the knife's cutting edge facing the plate.

- You will find the butter knife above and to the left of the place plate.

- The water glass is to the right of the place plate.

- As you use the butter knife to butter your bread—and remember to butter the bread as you eat it—the spent butter knife settles itself on the bread plate.

- The spoon is next, followed by the teaspoon, which is used for cream and sugar in your coffee cup or tea. The spent soup spoon is returned to the plate the soup bowl rests on.

- A small sterling silver fork above the charger plate is your dessert fork. You may then expect a cake dessert or, if you are dining in the United Kingdom, you may expect either cake or ice cream, as the English eat their ice cream as well as their cake with a fork!

- Saltcellar and pepper pot containers may be placed at individual place settings or a service of salt and pepper may be shared by a group of two persons at a dinner party. The rule for salt and pepper is simple. When someone asks for the salt, you pass the pepper, too, as salt and pepper are a team.

- You may find the napkin folded on your plate or on the right side of your plate to the right of the spoon, or it may be handed to you by the wait staff. When seated at the table, the first item immediately removed from the table is the napkin. It is placed in the lap.

- Candles add atmosphere to a beautifully decorated table. However, they are not used on breakfast or noon tables. Candles are used on a dining table when there is a lack of daylight.

- Flowers are placed in arrangements or in bowls and must not block the view of anyone at the table who wishes to converse with those across the table or at either end of the table.

- When hosting a dinner party for friends and guests, remember that the dining chairs are placed close to the table and not too close. Leave at least a finger-width of space between the table and top of the chair. Convenience is the key, so give an inch-and-a-half or two inches between the table and the top of the chair.

- A woman's handbag either rests on the woman's lap or is placed on the floor out of the path of the wait people and the other diners.

- When a man and woman are out together to dine and seated at a table, the woman is placed in the best light, so all who pass the table see her. When going to an evening event that includes dinner, it is customary for the couple to be seated at different tables from one another in order to share in different conversations. Being seated apart and with friends or new acquaintances adds to the conversation on the way home.

- When the meal is finished, the entree fork is placed on the plate in a specific fashion so the wait staff is alerted you have completed your meal. When the main meal is finished, the fork and knife are centered vertically on the plate. The sharp blade of the knife faces the fork.

- Most restaurants place the cream for coffee and tea in a container on the table along with sugar cubes in a bowl with a pincher. However, a restaurant may serve sugar in envelopes or in long, paper cylinders as opposed to cubes. Keep the table setting and its area tidy by tucking all sugar and sweetener wrappers and tiny, empty creamer containers under the dining plate.

- All food and food items are passed from your left around the table, as most people are right-handed. It is a time-honored formality.

## Eating Etiquette Challenges and Rules

**Holding the knife and fork American style:** In being taught to use the knife "American" style, a person should cut the meat into bite-sized pieces. Place the fork in the left hand with the prongs downward and held near the top of the handle. Place the index finger on the shank so it points to the prongs and is supported at the side by the thumb. The other fingers close underneath to hold the handle tight. The knife is in the right hand. Cut. Switch the knife to the edge of the plate and move the fork to the right hand, tine bend still down. Spear the cut portion and move to the mouth.

**Holding the knife and fork European style:** In the "European" method, the fork is most often held in the left hand, tine bend up. The knife never leaves the right hand and is often used to push the cut portion, or maybe a non-cut bite, onto the backside of the fork. The left hand then raises the fork, with tine bend still up, to the mouth. The knife is not placed on the plate's edge.

**Soup:** Soup noises are frowned upon. One eats cream soup with a soupspoon. If it is served in a bowl or drunk from a cup, then a clear soup may be consumed with a spoon. Do not blow on hot soup. Wait for it to cool. Dip your spoon away from you when you are eating soup. If the food in the soup is too large to eat in one bite, use the side of your spoon to cut the pieces into bite-size. A knife never belongs in a soup bowl. If you are served soup in a flat soup plate, leave the spoon in the plate when you are finished. If your soup comes in a cup or a bowl, the spoon is laid to rest on the plate that is under the cup or bowl.

**Eating with your hands:** You may consume tacos, fried chicken and pizza with your hands as well as bread, toast, dinner rolls, French fries and tortillas. Hamburgers, hot dogs, potato chips and pretzels also fall into this category.

**Pasta:** All pasta is eaten with a fork.

**Olives:** If the olive has a pit, simply cup your hand and fingers and very quietly spit the pit into your fingers. Place the pit on your salad plate or your bread and butter plate.

**Melons:** Watermelon is customarily eaten with a fork. Other melons are eaten with a fork unless they are served uncut in their rind. If they are served in their rind, they are eaten with a spoon.

**Artichokes:** Eat the leaves with the fingers and use a knife and fork for the heart.

**Bacon:** Although it is rather tempting to do so, do not eat bacon with your fingers! Bacon should be eaten with a knife and fork.

# Dining with Family

Just because you are dining with your family around the kitchen table, you can still observe courtesy and graciousness.

Make family mealtime an event that your family is eager to attend! Families that dine together tend to be more stable than those where meals are hit-or-miss. If your schedule does not allow time to have a meal all together every night, set one night a week for family dinner. Here are some tips for encouraging dining etiquette at mealtime.

- Set the table as if you were hosting friends. If possible, add flowers or a simple centerpiece. Remember that the flowers should be low on the table so as not to block views or conversations.

- Let everyone know what time dinner will be served and have them sit down at the table to eat.

- Turn off the television, unplug earphones and do not allow cell phones, computers and other electronic devices at the table.

- Practice table manners. Require children to say please and thank you and to properly pass food around the table.

- No matter how many people are at the table to eat, you may begin eating as long as two people have been served.

- Say grace, if appropriate, before beginning to eat.

- Encourage positive table talk and involve children in conversations.

- Do not clear the food from the table until everyone is finished.

- Clear all utensils, plates and serving dishes from the table before serving dessert and coffee.

## Business Luncheons

- Wear a garment that is clean and pressed.

- Have paper and pen with you unless the event has room for your laptop or tablet.

- Be sure to bring business cards.

- If the luncheon is to review specific material, have copies with you.

- Enjoy the meal.

- Leave your cell phone in your vehicle. There isn't anything as distracting as someone on their cell phone during a meeting, either placing a call or answering one.

- Send a thank you note within three days of the luncheon to your host, thanking your host for including you.

## Business Dinners

- If the dinner is a hosted event, you will receive an invitation. Respond to it whether or not you are attending.

- When you arrive, you may receive a program when you enter the room and directions to your table.

- Find the host or hostess to make your presence known.

- Have business cards with you but remember to line through your company's name on the card and write your name above it.

- Cell phones do not belong at dinner.

- If there is a guest speaker, introduce yourself to the guest speaker.

- If you know you will have to leave early, give your regrets to the guest speaker before the dinner festivities begin.

- If the event is an awards event and you are cited, be gracious and brief. Be sure to thank the audience.

- Send a thank you note within three days of the dinner to your host, thanking your host for including you.

For more business savvy see "Business Smarts" by Evelyn Lundström on page 61.

## Awards Ceremonies

- These events are always perfectly orchestrated and finely tuned.

- After giving your RSVP, arrange to arrive in a timely fashion.

- Leave the cell phone in the vehicle.

- Find a program and your correct seating arrangement.

- Next, greet the host or hostess and the guest speakers and VIPs.

- If you receive an award, be gracious and brief. Be sure to thank the appropriate people or entities including the audience.

- Send a thank you note within three days of the ceremony to your host or hostess, thanking your host or hostess for including you.

## Managing Awkward Moments

**Talking and chewing.** An important ingredient to the dining experience is conversation. Dining and conversation belong together. Naturally, we do not talk while the mouth is engaged in chewing. People sitting for a fine meal and fine conversation are aware that there will be short breaks in the patter.

**Excusing yourself from the table.** If you find you need to excuse yourself from the table, the formality is quite simple. Remove the napkin from your lap and say, "Please excuse me." You then get up from your chair and place the folded napkin to the right of your plate or you may fold it—soiled side in—and place it on the back of your chair. At no time does your napkin rest on your plate. When you return to the table, re-seat yourself, pick up the napkin and return it to your lap. Wait your turn to join the conversation.

**When food disagrees with you.** When you eat something with a fork or spoon and find that it does not agree with you, remove the food with the fork or spoon and return it to the plate. You may then excuse yourself from the table to find a restroom to rinse out your month.

## Etiquette Hints

•A woman may refresh her lipstick at the table. All other makeup is refreshed in the restroom.

- Sounds like burping or a growly stomach are unavoidable. Just say, "Excuse me." If someone else at the table does it, reply with a simple, "That's fine."

- If you must stop a drip from your nose, you may do so at the table by using a handkerchief or a piece of facial tissue in your handbag.

- Toothpicks need to be hidden from view. Couple your two hands around your mouth and place one hand on top of the other. Never dangle the toothpick out of the side of your mouth.

> *"There is only one corner of the universe you can be certain of improving, and that's your own self."*
> —Aldous Huxley, English writer

Choosing to follow the rules for dining is necessary for social polish and to set you apart from those who fail to respect the rules. Etiquette always has a positive effect on both you and those with whom you interact. When you know and practice the rules of dining etiquette, people will be eager to socialize with you, and you will be viewed as a gracious, generous host or hostess.

## ANITA SHOWER

*Etiquette is a life course.*
*You are the student.*

(805) 489-9696
anita@missetiquette.com
www.missetiquette.com

COMMENCING IN 1993, Miss Etiquette—Anita Shower—has made an impact on the newspaper, radio and television world. Her column, "Miss Etiquette," appears in the *SLO City News/Tolosa Press,* which is distributed on the Central Coast of California. You may hear her on talk show host Dave Congalton's radio program on KVEC 920 AM and as a radio personality on FOX Radio's *Sport Show* with Dan Murphy in Albany, New York. Miss Etiquette appears frequently on Rick Martel's *Rick at Night* television show in San Luis Obispo, broadcasting to thousands of people her answers to questions received from around the world via email and her popular website.

Anita hosts countless classroom discussions on etiquette and manners, and does training programs for Fortune 500® companies. In addition, you may find her presenting her student lecture series at the famous Madonna Inn or on the campuses of San Luis Obispo, Arroyo Grande and Nipomo high schools. She also has a children's program in San Luis Obispo.

Her courses are delivered with knowledge and conviction, and received with enthusiasm. Anita loves the subject of etiquette and remains a constant patron of the art of manners.

# Entertaining and Being the
## *Gracious* Host
### Life is a Celebration!

by Sharon Ringiér, PWC

PRIOR TO becoming a wedding and special event planner, I loved hosting my own parties and found any excuse to do so. Whether I planned birthday celebrations for my two sons, who are now twenty and twenty-four, Mother's Day brunch for my mother-in-law, holiday festivities for the family or my annual ornament exchange, I always felt the need to do it with "Martha Stewart flair."

There are so many opportunities to entertain and host at home. Do-it-yourself has created a new niche for all forms of entertaining. However, our lives are also busier than ever and taking time out of our busy schedules to plan any special soirée is a challenge.

In October 2010, my husband and I celebrated our twenty-fifth wedding anniversary, and we wanted to do something special for it. We were conflicted about how to incorporate something elegant with something simple. We wanted to include many of our friends for dinner and were on a budget. The larger concern was what type of party it would be if we had it at our house, which is a small two-bedroom townhouse. To add to the stress, we decided to plan this wonderful event with very little preparation time.

## Planning the Perfect Soirée

The advice that I have given my sons repeatedly throughout their lives is that the worst opportunity is a missed one. My motto is, "life is a celebration." You should never miss the opportunity to enjoy or celebrate it. Like I said, I look for any opportunity to celebrate. Planning a party should be as enjoyable as the party itself.

*"The most important thing is to enjoy your life—to be happy— it's all that matters."*
—Audrey Hepburn, British actress and humanitarian

The trick to planning the perfect party is understanding why you are celebrating, so I encourage you to set clear goals. I am extremely passionate about the planning process of a great party. Nothing makes a party more extraordinary than for you to make the celebration entertaining for your guest. Your celebration should tell a story from the moment your guests arrive.

**Make it memorable.** When my younger son, Kevin, graduated from high school, I wanted it to be a reflection of who he was as an individual. At the time, he was an airbrush artist for a local caricature company. I took his senior photo to the owner and asked if he could do a caricature of Kevin. When I received the finished product, the owner had exceeded my expectations by designing it with Kevin wearing his cap and gown. The artist had put a pencil signifying his artistic abilities in one hand and a diploma in the other, setting the tone of the celebration. I took this one element and threaded the concept throughout the entire party.

So many factors go into making your celebration memorable. Evaluate the celebration you are hosting. Regardless of what type of celebration it is, ask yourself what makes it special and unique. Above and beyond the obvious, guests remember things that fascinate them about parties. I am sure you can remember parties you attended that evoked a special feeling. Do you still talk about that party? When planning your next party, try to remember what excited you as well as what you did not like about past parties. Consider using this concept to develop your theme. By doing this, you will begin to tell your story.

**Add your own little, personal touches.** Nothing excites me more than to go to a party and see the personal touches that the hostess has added to make the party special. Therefore, when I start planning, I immediately think of what I can do to create the same feeling. Your guests will appreciate when you take the time to add special, little touches, which do not have to be expensive or elaborate. For example, I made chocolate peppermintinis for my annual ornament exchange this year. Instead of crushing peppermint to rim the glasses, I added little peppermint sticks to each drink to spruce up the look.

**Think about parting gifts.** I wanted each guest who attended my ornament exchange to receive a pair of rhinestone earrings as a "thank you" for being a part of my life. The gesture was simple, yet sweet and personal. Not sure what to give? Most people love sweets. Pick up small candy gifts from a local boutique. If you do not want to do sweets, give the gift of scented candles with a little message saying, "You light up my life."

Too often, we take our friends and family for granted. Consider having a welcoming committee to greet every person who walks in your door and say goodbye as they leave. I am a firm believer in walking every single person to the door.

**Create a mood that excites senses and inspires feelings.** The doorbell rings, and you open the door. What is the first thing your guest experiences when they enter the room? The way you greet your guest, the lighting when they walk in, and the fragrances they smell all set the mood for the entire evening. If the décor budget is minimal, you do not have to spend an exorbitant amount of money to create a warm and welcoming mood. Regardless of what type of social soirée you are hosting, there is always room for soft music and delicate smelling candles.

Have you ever sold a home? Realtors always encourage sellers to bake cookies or a cake to give a feeling of home. Why not use this concept for your entertaining purposes? Depending on the season, you can purchase candles or air fragrance products to be strategically placed throughout your home.

One of the things I am notorious for is burning candles, no matter what time of year it is. During the day when I am alone, I love to use them for the fragrance. However, when I am entertaining at home, I always have candles as part of my décor. When my husband and I celebrated our wedding anniversary, I wanted the ambiance to reflect my personality. I used candles throughout the house in a variety of ways—from votive candles in mini votive cups to large cylinder vases with floating candles—to create a warm and welcoming feeling.

**Cheers to you!** If you want to be remembered for being a fabulous hostess, extend the perfect toast! What better way to thank people for taking time out of their busy schedules and lives than to extend a warm welcome with a toast. Whether I go to dinner with friends, have them over for lunch or are just casually sitting around, if there is a glass with something being poured, I love to extend a toast to our continued friendship.

Here is my recipe for the perfect toast. Feel free to modify the recipe to fit your own personal style.

• Always introduce yourself. Make a point of getting everyone's attention and introduce yourself. Even though your friends know you, your guest may have someone with them who does not.

- Welcome them to your event. Again, it's all about presentation. Share something funny or comical to lighten things up a bit. I usually share what I almost burned that day in the kitchen!

- Close the toast by thanking everyone for coming and give well wishes on continued friendships and new ones.

## Planning with Very Little Time

In a perfect world, planning a party with three to six months to get organized is ideal. However, in my world, I have yet to plan any celebration with that much time. I tend to fly by the seat of my pants when I decide to host anything at my house. With best intentions in mind, I think about planning my celebrations with more than enough time, yet by the time I think about execution of the event, I have less than a month to really pull it all together.

**Create a plan of action.** No matter how much time you have, create a plan of action. Get organized and set parameters. Know what you want to accomplish. Let's say you want to have a tea for your bridge group. Envision what you would like to see happen. Then, define your purpose by thinking about adjectives that would describe the overall feel of your party. These few steps will help to create your theme and will give you a basis to start with. You can also start a binder and create tabs to categorize the planning process. Great tabs to start with can be theme/ideas, budget, guest list and vendors, just to name a few.

**Determine your budget.** Generally, when you are planning with a sense of urgency, you tend to spend more than is expected because you are under pressure to get things accomplished. Again, set parameters. The best way to not fall into the budget trap is:

- Determine how many guests you would like to invite and keep in mind that approximately one-fourth of them will not attend.

- Decide what type of food you would like to serve—for example, appetizers and light beverages or a plated meal.

- Decide whether you want to serve alcoholic beverages.

- Decide who to invite. Regardless of the type of party I am hosting, I always invite the friends who are effervescent and light up the room. These friends can help keep the party lively.

There are so many ways to invite guests these days. The beauty is that you do not need a lot of notice for some of these options.

- Evite.com® is a great website to invite your friends via email and on short notice.

- Email, while informal, has become more acceptable nowadays.

- Snail mail is, of course, the most formal yet much slower way.

Regardless of the method you decide to use, please take the time to call your guests. This is just a precautionary measure to make sure that everyone is informed in a timely manner.

## Planning for a Large Party in a Small Space

I planned our anniversary party for my small, two-bedroom town-house. What I did not mention was that I invited eighteen people for a sit-down dinner! That was an amazing feat to accomplish.

When you want to entertain at home and do not have the space to do so, get creative. Think about the flow of the party and repurpose your space. I converted my living room into a dining area room, my kitchen became the buffet, and the dining room housed the desserts and drinks. Make your biggest area the dining area. I wanted to have a formal dining experience. So, I moved all of my furniture into my garage and rented three six-foot tables, twenty fruitwood chairs and linens to create my dining area. I understand that not everyone has the luxury of moving furniture around. Your space will dictate the type of gathering you are able to host.

**Set up stations and décor to direct traffic.** I needed to hide part of a room for one of my son's birthday parties, and moving the furniture was not a practical option. I decided to hang simple fabric from the ceiling to block the area and discourage anyone from going in that area. Fabric draping is not just for weddings anymore!

Consider offering bite-sized food and creating food stations to keep guests where you want them.

**Buffet and bar.** What if you do not have enough space to create a bar or serving station? Once I used a door that was not hung, placed it on two sawhorses, covered it with plastic for protection and then with fabric as decor. That became my serving station for my fortieth birthday party.

At my anniversary party, I took a beveled glass shelf from my office and set it atop a bookcase in my dining room to use as a bar for drinks. I moved my dining room table off to the side to use as a gift table, stored all of the chairs in the garage and put the desserts on a card table in a corner of the room. This helped make the traffic flow easily as people served themselves.

## Finding the Right Resources

What you are trying to accomplish with your party will determine what resources you need to find.

**Food and beverages.** What you decide to do about this will make or break your event. Please keep in mind that neither has to be elaborate, just tasteful. I have gone to social events where they have served nothing more than appetizers and light refreshments. It was so elegant and refreshing.

Once your theme is determined, you can decide what refreshments would work best to accommodate the feel of the event. Many restaurants cater small events and parties and offer staffing services to meet your needs. When I hosted my son's graduation, I hired a bartender and server. I cannot describe how helpful this was when food needed to be replenished. If you decide to prepare the food yourself, there are great resources like Sam's Club® and Costco® that offer restaurant-quality appetizers. See also "Wine Savvy" by Jennifer L. Chou on page 173.

**Decor.** My favorite place to go for decorating ideas is Michaels®. They have some of the best resources for centerpieces and decorative tablescapes. You can also find great little decorative vases, votive cup holders and glass cylinders at stores like Walmart® and Target®. Even several of the dollar stores have great little finds.

**Rentals.** Rental companies can provide everything from tables and chairs to linens and china and are more than happy to work with you to help bring your vision to reality.

**Photography.** I am an advocate of capturing moments. I invited a photographer to my ornament exchange. When I saw the video montage she put together from the photos she had taken—moments that I did not realize had happened—it nearly brought me to tears. All of your hard work to organize a wonderful gathering, no matter how large or small, needs to be captured. It is a wonderful surprise when you reflect back on your party and see how happy people were.

Spend time thinking about what makes you unique and "you" before you start to plan your event. If the party is for someone else, what makes them unique and "them?" Capitalize on those qualities to design your event. Regardless of how many guests you invite, they will appreciate the effort and time you take to make it personal and intimate. No matter what happens, please remember that things are not going to be perfect and that is okay! What is most important is the smile on a loved one's face because you made the celebration about him or her and expressed your appreciation for having this person a part of your day.

Remember, life is a celebration!

**SHARON RINGIÉR,** PWC
**Sharon Ringiér Events**

*Your loyal partner for every occasion*

(847) 219-1080
sharon@sharonringier.com
www.sharonringier.com

KNOWN FOR her exuberant personality and can-do attitude, Sharon Ringiér is the proud owner of Sharon Ringiér Events. She has been married for 26 years and has renewed her wedding vows three times since her first wedding in October 1985.

Falling in love with the planning and production of her own wedding, Sharon decided to pursue a career as a wedding planner and in March 1997, received training from the Association of Certified Professional Consultants in San Jose, California. Her talents, desire to "relish in love" and determination has made her the spirited and fun loving coordinator and designer that she is today. For Sharon, life is a celebration and her goal is to help her clients celebrate and memorialize the events of their lives and loves.

Sharon's ability to design, create and envision, and her enthusiasm help her clients visualize and personalize their event from start to finish. She treats every event, every party and every wedding as if it were her first. Her skills and mastery of planning and producing have landed her in the celebrity scene planning the fabulous wedding of the world-renowned Blues artist Shemekia Copeland!

# Wine *Savvy*

## Business and Social Wine Smarts

### by Jennifer L. Chou

*H*AVE YOU ever entertained clients at a fancy restaurant and been overcome with WINEtimidation®? You know, you receive the wine list, and it is thicker than a volume of *War and Peace,* and you do not know where to begin. Should you order a bottle of a wine offered by the glass, or should you splurge to impress whom you are entertaining? Do you know why the server presents the bottle and what you are looking for? Do you know the proper way to taste wine and avoid looking like a fool?

Have you ever been asked to bring a bottle of wine to a friend's house or dinner party? Are you the hostess at the store looking at the sea of wine? Your blood pressure increases, and you are overwhelmed by the selections and a fear of picking a "bad" bottle. How much should you spend and will it overpower the food?

When I ask people how they feel about wine, most tell me they are intimidated by it, which is what made me think of the term *WINEtimidation—wīn·timi·dation—the lack of self-confidence in know- ledge about fermented grape juice.*

A few basic terms are needed to speak the language of wine.

- **Varietal** simply refers to the grapes as in Chardonnay grapes.

- **Vintage** is the year in which the grapes were grown and picked such as 2011. Some wines do not have a vintage because the winery uses wine from more than one year. Non-vintage wines are common in sparkling wines.

- **Body** is the weight of wine in your mouth. More on this later.

- **Tannins** are what you feel on the back of your tongue that can sometimes make you pucker. Heavier-bodied wines, such as Cabernet Sauvignon often have more tannin.

- **Acidity** is sometimes described as tart and actually makes your mouth water while tannins make it dry.

- **Legs,** sometimes referred to as tears, run down your glass after swirling the wine.

- **A corked bottle** of wine refers to a tainted bottle where oxygen or bacteria have affected the taste of wine. Corked wine usually smells like wet dog or newspaper.

## The Business Dinner that Impresses

Let's start with the business dinner. My good friend Jodi entertains clients all over the world and confided in me that she is not confident on selecting a wine to order when given the wine list. Sound familiar?

In this situation, there are two ways you can handle this: Defer to a wine lover at your table, if you have one, or look at wines offered by the glass and ask for a taste of a wine you are familiar with. In my wine workshops, I mention this tip and usually get a response of, "You can do that?" Yes, please do this!

Restaurants would prefer that you taste a couple of wines and be happy with your selection instead of buying a wine that you *might* like. If you happen to have a wine-savvy server, he or she can recommend a more expensive bottle based on what you liked and did not like. This tip has helped many professionals like Jodi discover their own palate and feel more confident ordering wine for a business dinner or even at a social function.

How much to spend on a bottle is up to you and your company's budget. The typical range is $50-$150 per bottle. I personally think $75 is conservative, yet allows you to wow your guests with a smart selection for a delicious bottle. Keep in mind you may need two or three bottles of wine depending on the size of your group. Figure one bottle for four people. For a dinner of eight people, you will definitely need two bottles.

Do you know why your server presents the bottle you ordered? Jodi had an "aha moment" regarding this topic when she came to one of my workshops where I presented two different bottles of red wine from the same winery that look identical. One was a Malbec and the other a Bonarda. The only difference was the color of the print on the bottle, which was not much bigger than what you are reading now. Can you imagine how easy it is for a server or bartender to accidentally pull the wrong bottle and open it if you do not catch that it is not the bottle you ordered?

Besides looking for the correct grape, you should also look at the vintage. This is especially true for expensive wines that are highly rated by magazines. One of the best examples of this is the 1997 versus 1998 vintage of Napa Valley Cabernet Sauvignon. The 1997 vintage was the vintage of the decade and delicious to drink right away. The 1998 vintage was not as lucky and had heavy tannins. The bottom line is that Mother Nature is different every year, and wines will vary from vintage to vintage.

**Smart tip.** Most restaurants allow you to bring in a bottle of wine for an opening *corkage* fee, usually $15 to $30 per bottle. Call ahead to ask and save embarrassment. In most states, you can take an open bottle home if you put it in your trunk.

Let's answer the last question about our business dinner: What is the proper way to taste? There are five steps to fully taste a wine.

**1. Look at the color against a white backdrop.** Color is a clue to how much body a wine will have and the wine's age. White wines can vary in color from almost clear to honey and become golden with bottle aging. Red wines range in color from a pale salmon to a deep purple, and over time, they lose color and have a brown undertone. In general, the more color a wine has, the heavier it will feel on your palate.

**2. Swirl your glass of wine to help it breathe.** Remember that this wine has been inside a bottle for at least a year and may need some time to open up and let its best qualities develop. Give the wine a good swirl in your glass, and you may notice the legs streaming down your glass. Thick legs indicate a full body wine with higher alcohol content.

To demonstrate how breathing changes a wine, I encourage you to open a bottle of red wine and taste it immediately. Then wait for an hour or two and taste it again. Usually, you will notice a big difference between the first taste and the second one after the wine has breathed for an hour.

**Smart tip:** When you are hosting, open your wine an hour before guests arrive. This will save last-minute rushing, and your wine will taste better.

**3. Stick your nose in the glass and let the aromas come through.** I know, you are thinking of the movie *Sideways* where Simon's nose is so far into his glass, you are certain it is stuck. You do not need to go to this extreme! Simply put your nose halfway in, so you can smell the bouquet of aromas. If you close your eyes, you will be more able to focus on your sense of smell and identify honeysuckle, blackberry jam, rose petals and so on. Remember that smell is seventy percent of how you taste anything.

**4. Take a small sip to cleanse your palate.** This will neutralize any strong tastes, such as blue cheese or barbeque pork, you just ate and prepare you for tasting the wine.

**5. Take a full sip, swish in your mouth and enjoy.** This is the moment you have been waiting for—actually enjoying the wine. Once you have a full taste in your mouth, you can choose to aerate the traditional way of breathing in through your mouth while the wine is in your mouth. Be careful! My friend nearly choked doing this, so I choose to close my mouth and swish in a front-to-back motion across my tongue. You are trying to detect new flavors and feel the body of the wine on your palate. Lastly, and most of all, enjoy this moment with wine! This is your ultimate goal: Find a wine you like and enjoy with clients, colleagues or friends.

# Personal Events

Now that we have some familiarity on wine speak and how to professionally taste and talk about wine at our business dinner, let's turn to a personal setting. Whether you are entertaining in your home or buying a bottle as a hostess gift, the wine shop can be overwhelming. How much should you spend and will it complement the food? Do you even know what is for dinner? See also "Entertaining and Being the Gracious Host" by Sharon Ringiér on page 163.

My rule of thumb for buying wine as a hostess gift is this: You can never go wrong with bubbles—Champagne, Cava, Prosecco, Moscato d'Asti, Sekt or sparkling wine in general. Wines labeled "sparkling" are often from California and range in quality and style.

• **Champagne** is the gold standard and has become synonymous with bubbles; however real Champagne is only produced in the region of Champagne, France.

- **Cava** is made in the same traditional method as Champagne. It is from Spain and uses different grapes.

- **Prosecco** is from Italy and typically not as bubbly as Cava.

- **Moscato** is light, sweet and the fastest growing type of wine today. Moscato d'Asti is a high quality wine and made near the town of Asti in Piedmont, Italy.

- **Sekt** is sparkling wine from Germany or Austria and not as well known as the others.

Why gift bubbles? Because you can enjoy them with virtually every part of the meal, and it pairs wonderfully with a wide range of food, particularly anything fried, salty, creamy or delicate. Even if everyone brought a bottle of bubbles as a gift, the hostess can choose to open now or save for later. As far as how much to spend, my gifting recommendation is a $15 to $20 bottle. Enough to purchase a quality wine, yet not bankrupt you.

## Food and Wine

This brings us to a question of common wines and how to pair them with food. First, I would like to highlight a few common grape varietals. Then we will cover food and wine pairing myths.

It is estimated that Italy alone has almost 1,000 different types of grapes! Below is a list of some of my favorite wines including grapes you are familiar with. I have listed these in order of lightest to heaviest weight in your mouth. To understand this order, we must discuss in detail the term *body*. Wine terms can be obscure and difficult to grasp. The easiest way to understand *body* is to compare wine to milk.

Let's look at milk varieties. There is skim, 1 percent, 2 percent, whole, half-and-half, cream and heavy cream. Most of us understand the difference in heaviness between skim milk and heavy cream in our mouth. The list below includes the milk weight to highlight the body of each wine.

## White Wines

- **Moscato d'Asti**—light and sweet with low alcohol (skim)

- **Riesling**—sweet with good acidity (varies, skim to 2%)

- **Chenin Blanc**—ranges from slightly sweet to crisp (1% to 2%)

- **Torrontes**—slightly sweet and medium body (2% to whole)

- **Pinot Grigio**—some fruit and nice acidity, can be dry (2% to whole)

- **Sauvignon Blanc**—dry, crisp like grapefruit in a glass (2% to whole)

- **Viognier**—a full, round wine with some fruitiness (whole to cream)

- **Chardonnay**—full body and most popular white wine (2% to heavy cream)

## Red Wines

- **Grenache**—light fruity red with almost no tannins (2%)

- **Pinot Noir**—light to medium body, somewhat earthy and dry (2% to half & half)

- **Sangiovese**—medium body, rustic, fruit and tannins (2% to half and half)

- **Malbec**—medium to full body, dark fruit, tannins (whole to cream)

- **Merlot**—fruit forward, medium body and tannins (half-and-half to heavy cream)

- **Syrah or Shiraz**—full body and fruity, can have heavy tannins (half-and-half to heavy cream)

- **Cabernet Sauvignon**—full body, structure and heavy tannins (half-and-half to heavy cream)

Since you have a good understanding of body and descriptions of a few types of wine, we can now discuss food and wine pairing rules. White wine with white meat and red wine with red meat, right? Wrong! My number one rule about food and wine pairings is that there are no rules. However, there are a few general rules, such as anything with a butter or cream sauce pairs nicely with a wine with acidity. Refer back to the body discussion of grapes and milk. A key to pairing is matching the body of wine with the weight of food.

Let's take an example of chicken. Chicken is very versatile and whether you make chicken picatta with a lemon butter sauce or chicken mole will determine which wine to drink. For chicken picatta, a Sauvignon Blanc or Chardonnay would be delicious. However, with the chicken mole, I would prefer a Pinot Noir or Malbec, which can stand up to the strong sauce. Ultimately, it comes down to your preferences. I might like Sauvignon Blanc, and you might not. It doesn't mean Sauvignon Blanc is bad. It means you probably don't like a wine with a lot of acidity.

Usually, a good wine shop will have a knowledgeable staff to help you with wine pairings. The best way to learn is experience, so start cooking and experimenting with wine pairings.

## Cold or Room Temperature?

Let's talk about temperature. White wines should be served ice cold, and red wines should be served at room temperature, right? Not necessarily. If you serve any wine ice cold, you will not taste the flavors. Serve most reds at room temperature or around 60 degrees Fahrenheit. For cellaring wine, the ideal temperature is 55 degrees Fahrenheit.

**Smart Tip.** Take white wine *out of the refrigerator* fifteen minutes before serving and put red wine *into the refrigerator* fifteen minutes before serving.

# Toasting

For all entertaining, it is important to know how to conduct a proper toast. There is a misconception that everyone needs to clink glasses no matter how far across the table they are. There are two main ways to toast that I feel are best. The first is for the host to state the toast and raise his or her glass. Then, without clinking, everyone raises their glass in the air and drinks in unison. For instance, "I would like to congratulate Donna on her promotion and thank you for celebrating with us tonight. Cheers!" Raise glass and drink in unison.

An alternative and fun way to toast is the *Circle of Friends*. In this scenario, the host says the toast, raises the glass and clinks the glass to the glass of the person on his or her right, who then clinks to his or her right until the toast circles back to the host who says, "Cheers." Then everyone raises their glass and takes a drink together. This requires a little coordination and is personally my favorite way to toast.

**Smart Tip.** Buy a book of toasts so you are never at a lack of words for special occasions. This was a gift for my friend Liz many years ago, and I refer to it often.

Now that you are smart and savvy on wine, go out to dinner with friends or clients and effortlessly ask for a taste of wine before ordering. Find a wine shop to explore and discover new wines. Bring a bottle of bubbles to your next dinner party, instead of your usual wine. Let all of your smart savviness bring grace and elegance wherever you go. Most of all, I want you to feel comfortable and confident about wine and conquer your WINEtimidation®.

**JENNIFER L. CHOU**
**Angel Share Wine Partners**

*Wine Education, Events & Tours to Help You Conquer Your WINEtimidation®*

(612) 205-5220
Jennifer@AngelShareWine.com
www.AngelShareWine.com

*C*HIEF WINE OFFICER Jennifer Chou is a ten-year wine industry veteran, who has had the great fortune to travel extensively in France, Italy, South Africa, California and Oregon. Her affinity with wine began at a young age since her grandparents' ordinary traditions included wine. A self-proclaimed "Wino and Foodie," her resume began in the music and financial industries. Serendipitous events led her to meet a winemaker and work with some of the most famous personalities in the wine world.

Jennifer started Angel Share Wine Partners for all those who fear the fermented grape. From exclusive bottle-signing events, drawing hundreds of people, to intimate winemaker dinners and wine workshops, Jennifer excels at working with organizations to create fun, customized, educational wine events and tours. She has participated in exclusive events such as Premiere Napa Valley,® Auction Napa Valley, Oregon Pinot Camp, Sun Valley Wine Auction and Vinitaly.

Jennifer lives in Minneapolis, Minnesota, with her family and two Boxer dogs. She is a member of the Magic Wand Collective, Women Entrepreneurs of Minnesota, Rotary International® and the Society of Wine Educators.

# Self-Change Through Self-*Love*

## Manifest the Body and Life of Your Dreams

by Kat Kim, CPC, ACE

WHAT IS your current story regarding your life, yourself, and your body? When you look in the mirror, what do you see?

If the answers to these questions are less than ideal and make you want to crawl under a rock, you are not the only one. According to the Social Issues Research Center, an organization that conducts research on social and lifestyle issues, eight out of ten women are unhappy with their physical appearance and will secretly admit that this dissatisfaction has an impact on both their personal and professional lives.

The great news is this: If you do not like your story, you have the power to change it!

The first thing to understand is that you are ultimately responsible for your life, your health and the way you look. By following the seven steps of my program, *Self-Change through Self-Love*,™ you will find the keys to change your story and live a life full of meaning and joy—while looking great from head to toe!

## Step One. Embrace your Image

Communication is always happening between you and the outer world through your image. The big misconception is that your image is all about your outer appearance. Though your appearance is important, it is only one piece of a much larger picture. Your image is actually composed of several interrelated components, which I call the *ABBC's of Image.*

**Appearance.** Your appearance is comprised of the type of clothing you wear, your accessories, hairstyle, makeup and overall physique. Through the way you dress and groom yourself, you communicate to the world whether you are conservative, casual, creative or sexy, along with a myriad of other personal traits.

**Body Language.** Body language includes your posture, eye contact, gestures, movements and facial expressions. Through your body language, you communicate signs of confidence, agreement and happiness, as well as signs of confusion, anger and dislike. You send and receive these body language cues almost entirely subconsciously, so, most of the time, you are communicating these feelings without even knowing it.

**Behavior.** We have all heard the saying, "Actions speak louder than words." Behavior represents actions and non-actions—the things you do or do not do—on a regular basis. Through behavior attributes, such as your attitude, humor and the way you treat others, you communicate volumes about what you may be thinking or feeling.

**Communication.** What you say and how you say it is the most obvious way to communicate. However, the way you speak your words through intonation, volume, speed and tone often bears more influence than the words themselves do.

You are also receiving messages from others through their image, as well. According to social psychologists, such as Dr. Frank Bernieri, who researches non-verbal communication at the University of Toledo in

Ohio, it takes less than thirty seconds for you to form an impression of someone you have just met because you are receiving messages through the ABBCs of their image. The constant communication that occurs between your image and the image of others becomes a point of attraction because you are either attracting people *to* you or repelling people *from* you through the messages you are sending.

**Question to ponder.** What is the message you want to send to others through your appearance, body language, behavior and communication? What do you want to attract into your life?

## Step Two. Understand Your Mindset

Your image is actually a direct reflection of your mindset. Your mindset begins with thoughts and beliefs. Every thought carries energy in the form of a feeling, or emotion, which directly affects your behavior. Your behavior results in your outcome.

**Thoughts and Beliefs** ▸ **Feelings** ▸ **Behavior** (words and actions) ▸ **Outcome**

This becomes a cycle because your outcome influences and reinforces your original thoughts and beliefs as shown in the mindset diagram below.

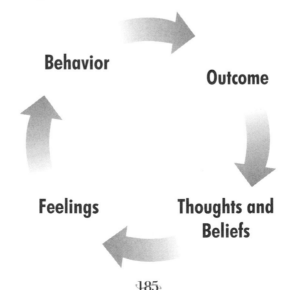

**Behavior**

**Outcome**

**Feelings**

**Thoughts and Beliefs**

Can you guess where your image is reflected in this diagram? The ABBCs of your image are all reflected in the "behavior" portion of your mindset. In other words, your behavior encompasses how you dress, how you act, what you say and how you say it. Your behavior, or overall image, directly influences your outcome or what you attract into your life.

From the mindset diagram, you can then see that your image is a direct manifestation of your thoughts and feelings and the communication that occurs through your image truly is your inner thoughts, beliefs and feelings.

What does this all mean? If you want to change your outcome (that is, lose weight, make more money, find balance and so on) and attract different things into your life, it is important to address the underlying thoughts and beliefs that are causing the current outcome. The root of your problem is not in what you do, it is in what you *think*.

In order to do this, there is one final piece to the mindset diagram I must show you (see diagram). A paradigm can be described as the way you see, perceive or understand something. Paradigms are the frame of reference in which you interpret your outcomes and tell the story of your life. *In order for real transformation to occur, you must first address your paradigms.*

Paradigms may sound like this:

• No matter how hard I try, I always fall short.

• I will never be as attractive as her.

• Life is a constant struggle because I am not smart enough.

As you can see from the mindset diagram on the next page, if you carry a paradigm that is based in self-criticism, loathe and lack, you will always interpret your outcome to support these negative paradigms. In other words, the story you tell will always be a negative one.

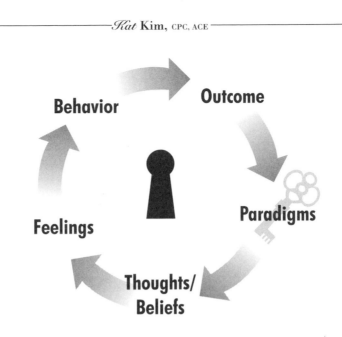

While paradigms require you to look for things to criticize in your life, new paradigms require you to look for beauty, abundance, love and health. Paradigms based in self-love may sound like this:

- My life is unfolding beautifully and I am right where I need to be.

- There is abundance and love wherever I look.

- My body responds remarkably well to healthy food and exercise.

*When you change the paradigm, your thoughts, beliefs, feelings, behavior and outcome all change.*

**Questions to ponder.** Looking through a paradigm of self-love, what are all the things that are working for you in your life? Where do you see beauty, abundance, love and health?

## Step Three. Get Clear on Your Core Values

Your core values are the essence of who you are. They are the things that are the most important to you on a very deep level. The quality of your life is most often directly related to the extent to which you honor them.

Here is an example of some values:

- Accomplishment
- Balance
- Beauty
- Compassion
- Contribution
- Family
- Freedom

- Leadership
- Nature
- Security
- Service
- Trust
- Wealth
- Wholeness

Living a value-based life from the inside out means that you are clear on what your top four to five values are, and you make your life choices based on what supports those values. Here are the main differences between living a value-based life from the inside out versus living from the outside in.

| Am I living my life from the . . . | **INSIDE-OUT** | or the . . . **OUTSIDE-IN** |
|---|---|---|
| **What are my influences?** | Core values | Society |
| | | Media |
| **Who decides what is important?** | I do | Friends |
| | | Family |
| | | Religion |
| **Who is in charge?** | I am | Others |
| **How do I make decisions?** | What do I feel about this? | |
| | Is this in alignment with my core values? | What will others think? |
| **What is the ultimate question?** | What will support my core values? | What if they don't agree/like? |
| | Does this feel right to *me*? | |

| Am I living my life from the . . . **INSIDE-OUT** | | or the . . . **OUTSIDE-IN** |
|---|---|---|
| **The action** | Be | Do do do. Burnout. Feel resentment. Continue to do do do. *OR* Do nothing |
| **The feeling** | Excitement, curiosity, fun, joy, alignment, ease, fulfillment, harmony, internal rightness, flow, resonance, satisfaction, love | Stuck, discomfort, discord, anger, tired, resentment, jealousy, stress, unhappy, sick, out of alignment |

As shown in the chart, you will know when you are living by your core values by how you feel. Following your core values brings you joy, ease and harmony, while disregarding them will have you feeling unhappy, stressed and out of alignment.

**Questions to ponder.** What are the top five joyful and wonderful life experiences you have had in your lifetime? What are the qualities of these peak experiences that made you feel so good?

# Step Four. Create a New Relationship to Your Body

While your core values are the inner, essential part of you, your body is the outer and external part of you. Your body is truly a gift of great magnitude, and it has been working for you since the time you were born. Yet so many people are disconnected from their bodies and have an extreme amount of dislike and shame towards the very thing that allows them to be.

Creating a new relationship to your body requires another paradigm shift that is based in love, respect and honor. It also means creating a new relationship to food and exercise.

*Honoring and respecting your body does not mean that you are stuck with the body you have.* It means you are connecting with your body and listening to its cues. The more you honor this new relationship, the more it will tell you exactly what it wants. You will find yourself naturally leaning toward healthy, whole foods and feeling the need for lots of movement. In other words, you will find yourself *easily transforming* the behavior (see mindset diagram on page 185) that you have been *struggling* to change all along.

**Questions to ponder.** What is your current relationship to your body, to food and exercise? What kind of relationship would you like it to be?

## Step Five. Learn How to Dress Yourself!

You can look inches taller, create a waist, hide your bulges and take off ten to fifteen pounds instantaneously—just by the garments you wear! You do not need to look or dress like a model to be stylish. Any woman at any age, size and budget can have great personal style.

A woman with personal style embraces her whole body, including what she does not like, and knows how to accentuate the parts she does love. Personal style comes from understanding:

• Your core values

• The message you want to send to others

• How you want to look and feel in your clothes

• Your body shape and coloring

• Personal style preferences

There is a wealth of information to help you understand how to dress for your body type, as well as many qualified stylists and image consultants who are eager to assist you in creating a wardrobe that fits your lifestyle and budget. Remember, not only is it important that you look and feel good in your clothes—you deserve to! See also "Your Image Matters—How and Why?" by Toby Parsons on page 13.

**Questions to ponder.** What types of styles and colors speak out to you? How do you want to look and feel in your clothes?

# Step Six. Write a New Story

Now it is time to physically write out a new story for how you want to look and feel. You will write it so it aligns with your core values, the physical health you want for your body and your personal style. Remember, the story you tell is the story you live. In all of the previous steps, I have listed questions to ponder that should help you get clearer on what you may want to include.

Here are some things to consider while writing your story:

- Start with a one-to-three year vision of how you would like to see yourself.

- Write the story in present tense, starting with "I am . . . ."

- Make sure to focus on the positive, not the negative. For example, instead of saying, "I don't want to be fat and unattractive," phrase it as, "I am healthy and beautiful."

- Keep the story short and easy to read.

- Remember to think big!

Here is an example of a before-and-after story of one of my clients:

**Before story:** "My life is a blur, and I don't really like to think about it. I am overwhelmed and broke. I am frustrated with my job, my body and myself. I know I have much more to offer, and when I look in the mirror, I see someone who is hiding. It's really disgusting. I don't like what I see."

**After story:** "I am strong, healthy and beautiful. My body loves fresh and whole foods. I love moving my body every single day, and it responds well to exercise. Life is fun and exciting! People recognize me for my power and authenticity, and I am financially free to do whatever I want!"

Once you have completed your story:

- Read it to yourself every morning and night before going to bed and as often as you can throughout the day.

- Close your eyes and imagine yourself in that story and feel the feelings you would have as if it were happening right now.

- Start doing this for thirty seconds throughout the day, particularly when you notice yourself feeling bad, and gradually increase the time to a maximum of five minutes.

- Pay attention to the inspired thoughts that come forth through this process.

The last step in this process will explain why it is so important to continually visualize yourself in your new story while feeling the good feelings.

## Step Seven. Be a Deliberate Thinker and Let Your Feelings Be Your Guide

**Everything is vibration.** Physicists, such as Niels Bohr, have discovered that all things in their purest and most basic forms consist of energy or vibrations. They have also discovered that all vibrations resonate at a certain level, and like attracts like in level of vibration. Thoughts also carry energy. If you refer back to the Mindset Diagram on page 185, you will see that when you think a thought, it will cause you to have a feeling. Feeling *is* vibration, and vibration *is* feeling.

**What you focus on expands and becomes your reality.** When you think a thought that makes you feel bad (low vibration), you will attract another thought that carries the same low vibration, and you will continue to feel bad. That thought will attract another of the same and soon enough these low vibrating, bad feeling thoughts will affect your behavior and then your outcome—what you manifest into your reality.

For example, if you consistently think that men do not like you because you are overweight and unattractive (your story), this will likely make you feel very sad. These feelings of sadness attract more of the same thoughts, and soon your disheartened mood triggers you to withdraw from others. Through your behavior and image, you communicate to others you are not available, so men do not like to approach you (outcome). Your story continues as you believe that men do not like you because you are overweight and unattractive.

The same is true of high vibrating, good feeling thoughts. The more good feeling thoughts you think, the more you will attract. These high vibrating, good feeling thoughts directly affect your behavior and, in turn, affect what you manifest into your life. Your thoughts truly become your reality. Since you have the power to choose what you think about in every moment, it is important to deliberately think good thoughts!

**Let your feelings be your guide.** According to the National Science Foundation, we have upwards of 50,000 thoughts per day. Managing every single one of these thoughts would be nearly impossible, so the key to leveraging attraction is by tuning into your feelings. Your feelings are a direct result of your thoughts, so you will know whether you are attracting and manifesting your old story or your new one by becoming more aware of what you are *feeling* in every moment.

**Pay attention to inspired action and behavior.** When you are in a good-feeling place, you will notice that you feel inspired to do something. These inspirations are higher vibration thoughts that you attract to yourself in your higher vibration-feeling place. Do you feel inspired to go for a walk or run a marathon? Maybe you suddenly feel interested in a book about how to start a business. Whatever it is, these inspirations will lead you with ease to the *behavior* that will bring you closer to the realization of your new story! That is how the Law of Attraction works!

**The story you tell is the story you live.** Go through these steps again and answer all the questions I have posed and create a story for your life that is absolutely joyous, abundant and beautiful. Keep focusing on that story with intention.

Let your feelings be your guide and always strive to feel good. Follow your inspirations. Love yourself. Honor and embrace your body. Adorn it with beautiful clothes that bring out your best features. Let your message to the world be that *you are absolutely magnificent!*

Because, my friend, *you are.*

**KAT KIM** CPC, ACE
**Revolution Self-Image**
**Entrepreneur, Workshop Leader & Speaker**

*Redefining beauty from the inside-out*

(206) 375-8098
Kat@revolutionselfimage.com
www.revolutionselfimage.com

*K*AT KIM is the founder and owner of Revolution Self-Image and creator of *Self-Change through Self-Love*™, a revolutionary seven-step process that is helping women across the world transform their lives and bodies. She is a nationally certified personal trainer, mindset coach, image consultant and Law of Attraction facilitator.

Kat's unique process is based on the philosophy that for lasting transformation to occur, you must first learn to love, honor and respect yourself. Formerly on the path to destruction and leading a very unhealthy life herself, Kat has used this same process to transform her life. She is now a very successful entrepreneur and a USA national level fitness competitor enjoying the life of her dreams.

Kat's vision is to start a global movement to redefine beauty from the inside out, so women and children all over the world can confidently look in the mirror and love the image they see. She speaks nationally and teaches others why self-love is so important to achieving personal and professional goals.

# MORE Socially Smart & Savvy

Now that you have learned many things about how to become socially smart and savvy with a wide variety of tips, techniques and strategies, the next step is to take action. Get started applying what you have learned in the pages of this book.

We want you to know that we are here to help you meet your professional and personal objectives. Below is a list of where we are geographically located. Regardless of where our companies are located, many of us provide a variety of services over the phone or through webinars, and we welcome the opportunity to travel to your location.

You can find out more about each of us by reading our bios at the end of our chapters, or by visiting our websites listed on the next pages. When you are ready for one-on-one consulting or group training from any of the co-authors in this book—we are available! If you call us and let us know you have read our book, we will provide you with a free phone consultation to determine your needs and how we can best serve you.

# *United States*

## California
Rachel Estelle                    www.socialmixology101.com
Karen Kennedy                    www.ladyblossoms.net
Caterina Rando                    www.caterinarando.com
Anita Shower                    www.missetiquette.com

## Colorado
Linnore Gonzales                    www.decorandyouhr.com

## Illinois
Sharon J. Geraghty                    www.labellafigura.com
Sharon Ringiér                    www.sharonringier.com

## Maryland
Margaret E. Jackson                    www.phenomenalbutterfly.com
Veronica T. H. Purvis                    www.veraiconica.com
Katrina Van Dopp                    www.katrinavandopp.com

## Minnesota
Jennifer L. Chou                    www.angelsharewine.com

## Texas
Thea Wood                    www.theawood.com

## Washington
Kat Kim                    www.revolutionselfimage.com
Toby Parsons                    www.iyimage.com

## Australia

Annalisa Armitage          www.myimageconsultant.com.au
Evelyn Lundström         www.firstimpressions.com.au

## Canada

Pankaj Sabharwal          www.style-guru.com
Shai Thompson          www.shaithompson.com

# *You're* Invited. . .

. . .to join us for any of our Sought After Speaker Summits!

**Do you have a message you want to share?**
**Are you ready to improve your speaking skills?**
**Have you seen how much influence people who speak have?**
**Would you like be a sought-after speaker?**

In one weekend you can develop your public speaking skills and be loud and proud about the value you bring. Join us for our next live event at: www.soughtafterspeaker.com

Because you are savvy enough to pick up this book we have a gift for you. Enter coupon code SASVIP50 for a 50% discount on your registration. Attend this event and watch how your social status climbs!

# Become a *Published* Author
# with THRIVE Publishing™

THRIVE Publishing develops books for experts who want to share their knowledge with more and more people. We can help you become a published author to showcase your expertise, build your list and advance your business and career.

We realize that getting a book written and published is a huge undertaking, and we make that process as easy as possible. We have an experienced team of professionals with the resources and knowledge to put a quality, informative book in your hands quickly and affordably.

We also partner with organizations or institutions to publish books that would be of interest to their members. In this case, sales of the book can be a revenue stream/fundraiser for the organization. A book can enhance your mission, give you a professional outreach tool and enable you to communicate essential information to a wider audience.

# Also from
# THRIVE Publishing™

Contact us to discuss how we can work together
on *your* book project.

Phone: **415-668-4535**
email: **info@thrivebooks.com**

# Also from
# THRIVE Publishing™

For more information
on this book, visit:
**www.inspiredstylebook.com**

For more information
on this book, visit:
**www.mystylemywaybook.com**

# Also from
# THRIVE Publishing™

For more information
on this book, visit:
**www.executiveimagebook.com**

For more information
on this book, visit:
**www.savvyleadershipbook.com**

# Also from
# THRIVE Publishing™

For more information
on this book, visit:
**www.powerofcivilitybook.com**

For more information
on this book, visit:
**www.connectionscountbook.com**

# Also from
# THRIVE Publishing™

For more information
on this book, visit:
**www.getorganizedtodaybook.com**

For more information
on this book, visit:
**www.powertochangebook.com**